Selected Addresses of Frederick Douglass

©2008 Wilder Publications

Wilder Publications, LLC.
PO Box 3005
Radford VA 24143-3005

ISBN 10: 1-60459-238-9
ISBN 13: 978-1-60459-238-2

T0018743

Table Of Contents

The Meaning of July Fourth for the Negro

Rochester, by Frederick Douglass, July 5th, 1852.

Mr. President, Friends and Fellow Citizens :

He who could address this audience without a quailing sensation, has stronger nerves than I have. I do not remember ever to have appeared as a speaker before any assembly more shrinkingly, nor with greater distrust of my ability, than I do this day. A feeling has crept over me, quite unfavorable to the exercise of my limited powers of speech. The task before me is one which requires much previous thought and study for its proper performance. I know that apologies of this sort are generally considered flat and unmeaning. I trust, however, that mine will not be so considered. Should I seem at ease, my appearance would much misrepresent me. The little experience I have had in addressing public meetings, in country school houses, avails me nothing on the present occasion.

The papers and placards say, that I am to deliver a 4th July oration. This certainly, sounds large, and out of the common way, for me. It is true that I have often had the privilege to speak in this beautiful Hall, and to address many who now honor me with their presence. But neither their familiar faces, nor the perfect gage I think I have of Corinthian Hall, seems to free me from embarrassment.

The fact is, ladies and gentlemen, the distance between this platform and the slave plantation, from which I escaped, is considerable — and the difficulties to be overcome in getting from the latter to the former, are by no means slight. That I am here today, is, to me, a matter of astonishment as well as of gratitude. You will not, therefore, be surprised, if in what I have to say, I evince no elaborate preparation, nor grace my speech with any high sounding exordium. With little experience and with less learning, I have been able to throw my thoughts hastily and imperfectly together; and trusting to your patient and generous indulgence, I will proceed to lay them before you.

This, for the purpose of this celebration, is the 4th of July. It is the birthday of your National Independence, and of your political freedom. This, to you, is what the Passover was to the emancipated people of God. It carries your minds back to the clay, and to the act of your great deliverance; and to the signs, and to the wonders, associated with that act that day. This celebration also marks the beginning of another year of your national life; and reminds you that the Republic of America is now 76 years old. I am glad, fellow-citizens, that your nation is so young. Seventy-six years, though a good old age for a man, is but a mere speck in the life of a nation. 'Three score years and ten is the allotted time for individual men; but nations number their years by thousands. According to this fact, you are, even now only in the beginning of you national career, still ling ering in the period of childhood. I repeat, I am glad this is so. There is hope in the thought, and hope is much needed, under the dark clouds which lower above the horizon. The eye of the reformer is met with angry flashes, portending disastrous times; but his heart may well beat lighter at the thought that America is young, and that she is still in the impressible stage of her existence. May he not hope that high lessons of wisdom, of justice and of truth, will yet give direction to her destiny? Were the nation older, the patriot's heart might be sadder, and the reformer's brow heavier. Its future might be shrouded in gloom, and the hope of its prophets go out in sorrow. There is consolation in the thought, that America is young.—Great streams are not easily turned from channels, worn deep in the course of ages. They may sometimes rise in quiet and stately majesty, and inundate the land, refreshing and fertilizing the earth with their mysterious properties. They may also rise in wrath and fury, and bear away, on their angry waves, the accumulated wealth of years of toil and hardship. They, however, gradually flow back to the same old channel, and flow on as serenely as ever. But, while the river may not be turned aside, it may dry up, and leave nothing behind but the withered branch, and the unsightly rock, to howl in the abyss—sweeping wind, the sad tale of departed glory. As with rivers so with nations.

Fellow-citizens, I shall not presume to dwell at length on the associations that cluster about this day. The simple story of it is, that, 76 years ago, the people of this country were British subjects. The style and title of your "sovereign people" (in which you now glory) was not then born. You were under the British Crown. Your fathers esteemed the English Government as the home government and England as the fatherland. This home government, you know, although a considerable distance from your home, did, in the exercise of its parental prerogatives, impose upon its colonial children, such restraints, burdens and limitations, as, in its mature judgment, it deemed wise, right and proper.

But, your fathers, who had not adopted the fashionable idea of this day, of the infallibility of government, and the absolute character of its acts, presumed to differ from the home government in respect to the wisdom and the justice of some of those burdens and restraints. They went so far in their excitement as to pronounce the measures of government unjust, unreasonable, and oppressive, and altogether such as ought not to be quietly submitted to. I scarcely need say, fellow-citizens, that my opinion of those measures fully accords with that of your fathers. Such a declaration of agreement on my part, would not be worth much to anybody. It would, certainly, prove nothing, as to what part I might have taken, had I lived during the great controversy of 1776. To say now that America was right, and England wrong, is exceedingly easy. Everybody can say it; the dastard, not less than the noble brave, can flippantly discant on the tyranny of England towards the American Colonies. It is fashionable to do so; but there was a time when, to pronounce against England, and in favor of the cause of the colonies, tried men's souls. They who did so were accounted in their day, plotters of mischief, agitators and rebels, dangerous men. To side with the right, against the wrong, with the weak against the strong, and with the oppressed against the oppressor! here lies the merit, and the one which, of all others, seems un fashionable in our day. The cause of liberty may be stabbed by the men who glory in the deeds of your fathers. But, to proceed.

Feeling themselves harshly and unjustly treated, by the home government, your fathers, like men of honesty, and men of spirit, earnestly sought redress. They petitioned and remonstrated; they did so in a decorous, respectful, and loyal manner. Their conduct was wholly unexceptionable. This, however, did not answer the purpose. They saw themselves treated with sovereign indifference, coldness and scorn. Yet they persevered. They were not the men to look back.

As the sheet anchor takes a firmer hold, when the ship is tossed by the storm, so did the cause of your fathers grow stronger, as it breasted the chilling blasts of kingly displeasure. The greatest and best of British statesmen admitted its justice, and the loftiest eloquence of the British Senate came to its support. But, with that blindness which seems to be the unvarying characteristic of tyrants, since Pharoah and his hosts were drowned in the Red sea, the British Government persisted in the exactions complained of.

The madness of this course, we believe, is admitted now, even by England; but , we fear the lesson is wholly lost on our present rulers.

Oppression makes a wise man mad. Your fathers were wise men, and if they did not go mad, they became restive under this treatment. They felt themselves the victims of grievous wrongs, wholly incurable in their colonial capacity. With brave men there is always a remedy for oppression. Just here, the idea of a total separation of the colonies from the crown was born! It was a startling idea, much more so, than we, at this distance of time, regard it. The timid and the prudent (as has been intimated) of that day, were, of course, shocked and alarmed by it.

Such people lived then, had lived before, and will, probably, ever have a place on this planet; and their course, in respect to any great change, (no matter how great the good to be attained, or the wrong to be redressed by it,) may be calculated with as much precision as can be the course of the stars. They hate all changes, but silver, gold and copper change! Of this sort of change they are always strongly in favor.

These people were called tories in the days of your fathers; and the appellation, probably, conveyed the same idea that is meant by a more modern, though a somewhat less euphonious term, which we often find in our papers, applied to some of our old politicians.

Their opposition to the then dangerous thought was earnest and powerful; but, amid all their terror and affrighted vociferations against it, the alarming and revolutionary idea moved on, and the country with it.

On the 2d of July, 1776, the old Continental Congress, to the dismay of the lovers of ease, and the worshippers of property, clothed that dreadful idea with all the authority of national sanction. They did so in the form of a resolution; and as we seldom hit upon resolutions, drawn up in our day, whose transparency is at all equal to this, it may refresh your minds and help my story if I read it.

Resolved, That these united colonies are, and of right, ought to be free and Independent States; that they are absolved from all allegiance to the British Crown; and that all political connection between them and the State of Great Britain is, and ought to be, dissolved.

Citizens, your fathers Made good that resolution. They succeeded; and today you reap the fruits of their success. The freedom gained is yours; and you, therefore, may properly celebrate this anniversary. The 4th of July is the first great fact in your nation's history-the very ring-bolt in the chain of your yet undeveloped destiny.

Pride and patriotism, not less than gratitude, prompt you to celebrate and to hold it in perpetual remembrance. I have said that the Declaration of Independence is the *Ringbolt* to the chain of your nation's destiny; so, indeed, I regard it. The principles contained in that instrument are saving principles. Stand by those principles, be true to them on all occasions, in. all places, against all foes, and at whatever cost.

From the round top of your ship of state, dark and threatening clouds may be seen. Heavy billows, like mountains in the distance, disclose to the leeward huge forms of flinty rocks! That bolt drawn, that chain, broken, and all is lost. Cling to this day-cling to it, and to its principles, with the grasp of a storm-tossed mariner to a spar at midnight.

The coining into being of a nation, in any circumstances, is an interesting event. But, besides general considerations, there were peculiar circumstances which make the advent of this republic an event of special attractiveness.

The whole scene, as I look back to it, was simple, dignified and sublime.

The population of the country, at the time, stood at the insignificant number of three millions. The country was poor in the munitions of war. The population was weak and scattered, and the country a wilderness unsubdued. There were then no means of concert and combination, such as exist now. Neither steam nor lightning had then been reduced to order and discipline. From the Potomac to the Delaware was a journey of many days. Under these, and innumerable other disadvantages, your fathers declared for liberty and independence and triumphed.

Fellow Citizens, I am not wanting in respect for the fathers of this republic. The signers of the Declaration of Independence were brave men. They were great men too-great enough to give fame to a great age. It does not often happen to a nation to raise, at one time, such a number of truly great men. The point from which I am compelled to view them is not, certainly the most favorable; and yet I cannot contemplate their great deeds with less than admiration. They were statesmen, patriots and heroes, and for the good they did, and the principles they contended for, I will unite with you to honor their memory.

They loved their country better than their own private interests; and, though this is not the highest form of human excellence, all will concede that it is a rare virtue, and that when it is exhibited, it ought to command respect. He who will, intelligently, lay down his life for his country, is a man whom it is not in human nature to despise. Your fathers staked their lives, their fortunes, and their sacred honor, on the cause of their country. In their admiration of liberty, they lost sight of all other interests.

They were peace men; but they preferred revolution to peaceful submission to bondage. They were quiet men; but they did not shrink from agitating against oppression. They showed forbearance; but that they knew its limits. They believed in order; but not in the order of tyranny. With them, nothing was "settled" that was not right. With them, justice, liberty and humanity were "final;" not slavery and oppression. You may well cherish the memory of such men. They were great in their day and generation. Their solid manhood stands out the more as we contrast it with these degenerate times.

How circumspect, exact and proportionate were all their movements! How unlike the politicians of an hour! Their statesmanship looked beyond the passing moment, and stretched away in strength into the distant future. They seized upon eternal principles, and set a glorious example in their defence. Mark them!

Fully appreciating the hardships to be encountered, firmly believing in the right of their cause, honorably inviting the scrutiny of an on-looking world, reverently appealing to heaven to attest their sincerity, soundly comprehending the solemn responsibility they were about to assume, wisely measuring the terrible odds against them, your fathers, the fathers of this republic, did, most deliberately, under the inspiration of a glorious patriotism, and with a sublime faith in the great principles of justice and freedom, lay deep, the corner-stone of the national super-structure, which has risen and still rises in grandeur around you.

Of this fundamental work, this day is the anniversary. Our eyes are met with demonstrations of joyous enthusiasm. Banners and penants wave exultingly on the breeze. The din of business, too, is hushed. Even mammon seems to have quitted his grasp on this day. The ear-piercing fife and the stirring drum unite their accents with the ascending peal of a thousand church bells. Prayers are made, hymns are sung, and sermons are preached in honor of this day; while the quick martial tramp of a great and multitudinous nation, echoed back by all the hills, valleys and mountains of a vast continent, bespeak the occasion one of thrilling and universal interest—a nation's jubilee.

Friends and citizens, I need not enter further into the causes which led to this anniversary. Many of you understand them better than I do. You could instruct me in regard to them. That is a branch of knowledge in which you feel, perhaps, a much deeper interest than your speaker. The causes which led to the separation of the colonies from the British crown have never lacked for a tongue. They have all been taught in your common schools, narrated at your firesides, unfolded from your pulpits, and thundered from your legislative halls, and are as familiar to you as household words. They form the staple of your national poetry and eloquence.

I remember, also, that, as a people, Americans are remarkably familiar with all facts which make in in their own favor. This is esteemed by some as a national trait—perhaps a national weakness. It is a fact, that whatever makes for the wealth or for the reputation of Americans, and can be had cheap! will be found by Americans. I shall not be charged with slandering Americans, if I say I think the Americans can side of any question may be safely left in American hands.

I leave, therefore, the great deeds of your fathers to other gentlemen whose claim to have been regularly descended will be less likely to be disputed than mine!

The Present

My business, if I have any here today, is with the present. The accepted time with God and his cause is the ever-living now.

"Trust no future, however pleasant, Let the dead past bury its dead; Act, act in the living present, Heart within, and God overhead."

We have to do with the past only as we can make it useful to the present and to the future. To all inspiring motives, to noble deeds which can be gained from the past, we are welcome. But now is the time, the important time. Your fathers have lived, died, and have done their work, and have done much of it well. You live and must die, and you must do your work. You have no right to enjoy a child's share in the labor of your fathers, unless your children are to be blest by your labors. You have no right to wear out and waste the hard-earned fame of your fathers to cover your indolence. Sydney Smith tells us that men seldom eulogize the wisdom and virtues of their fathers, but to excuse some folly or wickedness of their own. This truth is not a doubtful one. There are illustrations of it near and remote, ancient and modern. It was fashionable, hundreds of years ago, for the children of Jacob to boast, we have "Abraham to our father," when they had long lost Abraham's faith and spirit. That people contented themselves under the shadow of Abraham's great name, while they repudiated the deeds which made his name great. Need I remind you that a similar thing is being done all over this country today? Need I tell you that the Jews are not the only people who built the tombs of the prophets, and garnished the sepulchres of the righteous? Washington could not die till he had broken the chains of his slaves. Yet his monument is built up by the price of human blood, and the traders in the bodies and souls of men, shout—" We have Washington to "our father."—A las! that it should be so; yet so it is.

"The evil that men do, lives after them, The good is oft interred with their bones."

Fellow-citizens, pardon me, allow me to ask, why am I called upon to speak here today? What have I, or those I represent, to do with your national independence? Are the great principles of political freedom and of natural justice, embodied in that Declaration of Independence, extended to us? and am I, therefore, called upon to bring our humble offering to the national altar, and to confess the benefits and express devout gratitude for the blessings resulting from your independence to us?

Would to God, both for your sakes and ours, that an affirmative answer could be truthfully returned to these questions! Then would my task be light, and my burden easy and delightful. For who is there so cold, that a nation's sympathy could not warm him? Who so obdurate and dead to the claims of gratitude, that would not thankfully acknowledge such priceless benefits? Who so stolid and selfish, that would not give his voice to swell the hallelujahs of a nation's jubilee, when the chains of servitude had been torn from his limbs? I am not that man. In a case like that, the dumb might eloquently speak, and the "lame man leap as an hart."

But, such is not the state of the case. I say it with a sad sense of the disparity between us. I am not included within the pale of this glorious anniversary! Your high independence only reveals the immeasurable distance between us. The blessings in which you, this day, rejoice, are not enjoyed in common.—The rich inheritance of justice, liberty, prosperity and independence, bequeathed by your fathers, is shared by you, not by me. The sunlight that brought life and healing to you, has brought stripes and death to me. This Fourth July is yours, not mine. You may rejoice, I must mourn. To drag a man in fetters into the grand illuminated temple of liberty, and call upon him to join you in joyous anthems, were inhuman mockery and sacrilegious irony. Do you mean, citizens, to mock me, by asking me to speak today? If so, there is a parallel to your conduct. And let me warn you that it is dangerous to copy the example of a nation whose crimes, towering up to heaven, were thrown down by the breath of the Almighty, burying that nation in irrecoverable ruin! I can today take up the plaintive lament of a peeled and woe-smitten people!

" By the rivers of Babylon, there we sat down. Yea! we wept when we remembered Zion. We hanged our harps upon the willows in the midst thereof. For there, they that carried us away captive, required of us a song; and they who wasted us required of us mirth, saying, Sing us one of the songs of Zion. How can we sing the Lord's song in a strange land? If I forget thee, 0 Jerusalem, let my right hand forget her cunning. If I do not remember thee, let my tongue cleave to the roof of my mouth."

Fellow citizens; above your national, tumultuous joy, I hear the mournful wail of millions! whose chains, heavy and grievous yesterday, are, today, rendered more intolerable by the jubilee shouts that reach them. If I do forget, if I do not faithfully remember those bleeding children of sorrow this day, "may my right hand forget her cunning, and may my tongue cleave to the roof of my mouth!" To forget them, to pass lightly over their wrongs, and to chime in with the popular theme, would be treason most scandalous and shocking, and would make me a reproach before God and the world. My subject, then, fellow-citizens, is *American Slavery*. I shall see, this day, and its popular characteristics, from the slave's point of view. Standing, there, identified with the American bondman, making his wrongs mine, I do not hesitate to declare, with all my soul, that the character and conduct of this nation never looked blacker to me than on this 4th of July! Whether we turn to the declarations of the past, or to the professions of the present, the conduct of the nation seems equally hideous and revolting. America is false to the past, false to the present, and solemnly binds herself to be false to the future. Standing with God and the crushed and bleeding slave on this occasion, I will, in the name of humanity which is outraged, in the name of liberty which is fettered, in the name of the constitution and the Bible, which are disregarded and trampled upon, dare to call in question and to denounce, with all the emphasis I can command, everything that serves to perpetuate slavery—the great sin and shame of America! "I will not equivocate; I will not excuse;" I will use the severest language I can command; and yet not one word shall escape me that any man, whose judgment is not blinded by prejudice, or who is not at heart a slaveholder, shall not confess to be right and just.

But I fancy I hear some one of my audience say, it is just in this circumstance that you and your brother abolitionists fail to make a favorable impression on the public mind. Would you argue more, and denounce less, would you persuade more, and rebuke less, your cause would be much more likely to succeed. But, I submit, where all is plain there is nothing to be argued. What point in the anti-slavery creed would you have me argue? On what branch of the subject do the people of this country need light? Must I undertake to prove that the slave is a man? That point is conceded already. Nobody doubts it. The slave-holders themselves acknowledge it in the enactment of laws for their government. They acknowledge it when they punish disobedience on the part of the slave. There are seventy-two crimes in the State of Virginia, which, if committed by a black man, (no matter how ignorant he be,) subject him to the punishment of death; while only two of the same crimes will subject a white man to the like punishment.—What is this but the acknowledgement that the slave is a moral, intellectual and responsible being. The manhood of the slave is conceded. It is admitted in the fact that Southern statute books are covered with enactments forbidding, under severe fines and penalties, the teaching of the slave to read or to write.—When you can point to any such laws, in reference to the beasts of the field, then I may consent to argue the manhood of the slave. When the dogs in your streets, when the fowls of the air, when the cattle on your hills, when the fish of the sea, and the reptiles that crawl, shall be unable to distinguish the slave from a brute, then will I argue with you that the slave is a man

For the present, it is enough to affirm the equal manhood of the negro race. Is it not astonishing that, while we are ploughing, planting and reaping, using all kinds of mechanical tools, erecting houses, constructing bridges, building ships, working in metals of brass, iron, copper, silver and gold; that, while we are reading, writing and cyphering, acting as clerks, merchants and secretaries, having among us lawyers, doctors, ministers, poets, authors, editors, orators and teachers; that, while we are engaged in all manner of enterprises common to other men, digging gold in California, capturing the whale in the Pacific, feeding sheep and cattle on the hillside, living, moving, acting, thinking, planning, living in families as husbands, wives and children, and, above all, confessing and worshipping the Christian's God, and looking hopefully for life and immortality beyond the grave, we are called upon to prove that we are men!

Would you have me argue that man is entitled to liberty? that he is the rightful owner of his own body? You have already declared it. Must I argue the wrongfulness of slavery? Is that a question for Republicans? Is it to be settled by the rules of logic and argumentation, as a matter beset with great difficulty, involving a doubtful application of the principle of justice, hard to be understood? How should I look today, in the presence of Americans, dividing, and subdividing a discourse, to show that men have a natural right to freedom? speaking of it relatively, and positively, negatively, and affirmatively. To do so, would be to make myself ridiculous, and to offer an insult to your understanding.—There is not a man beneath the canopy of heaven, that does not know that slavery is wrong for him.

What, am I to argue that it is wrong to make men brutes, to rob them of their liberty, to work them without wages, to keep them ignorant of their relations to their fellow men, to beat them with sticks, to flay their flesh with the lash, to load their limbs with irons, to hunt them with dogs, to sell them at auction, to sunder their families, to knock out their teeth, to burn their flesh, to starve them into obedience and submission to their masters? Must I argue that a system thus marked with blood, and stained with pollution, is wrong? No I will not. I have better employment for my time and strength, than such arguments would imply.

What, then, remains to be argued? Is it that slavery is not divine; that God did not establish it; that our doctors of divinity are mistaken? There is blasphemy in the thought. That which is inhuman, cannot be divine! Who can reason on such a proposition? They that can, may; I cannot. The time for such argument is past.

At a time like this, scorching irony, not convincing argument, is needed. O! had I the ability, and could I reach the nation's ear, I would, to day, pour out a fiery stream of biting ridicule, blasting reproach, withering sarcasm, and stern rebuke. For it is not light that is needed, but fire; it is not the gentle shower, but thunder. We need the storm, the whirlwind, and the earthquake. The feeling of the nation must be quickened; the conscience of the nation must be roused; the propriety of the nation must be startled; the hypocrisy of the nation must be exposed; and its crimes against God and man must be proclaimed and denounced.

What, to the American slave, is your 4th of July? I answer; a day that reveals to him, more than. all other days in the year, the gross injustice and cruelty to which lie is the constant victim. To him, your celebration is a sham; your boasted liberty, an unholy license; your national great-ness, swelling vanity; your sounds of rejoicing are empty and heartless; your denunciations of tyrants, brass fronted impudence; your shouts of liberty and equality, hollow mockery; your prayers and hymns, your sermons and thanksgivings, with all your religious parade, and solemnity, are, to him, mere bombast, fraud, deception, impiety, and hypocrisy—a thin veil to cover up crimes which would disgrace a nation of savages. There is not a nation on the earth guilty of practices, more shocking and bloody, than are the people of these United States, at this very hour.

Go where you may, search where you will, roam through all the monarchies and despotisms of the old world, travel through South America, search out every abuse, and when you have found the last, lay your facts by the side of the every day practices of this nation, and you will say with me, that, for revolting barbarity and shameless hypocrisy, America reigns without a rival.

The Internal Slave Trade

Take the American slave-trade, which we are told by the papers, is especially prosperous just now. Ex-Senator Benton tells us that the price of men was never higher than now. He mentions the fact to show that slavery is in no danger. This trade is one of the peculiarities of American institutions. It is carried on in all the large towns and cities in one half of this confederacy; and millions are pocketed every year, by dealers in this horrid traffic. In several states, this trade is a chief source of wealth. It is called (in contradistinction to the foreign slave-trade) "the internal slave-trade." It is, probably, called so, too, in order to divert from it the horror with which the foreign slave-trade is contemplated. That trade has long since been denounced by this government, as piracy. It has been denounced with burning words, from the high places of the nation, as an execrable traffic. To arrest it, to put an end to it, this nation keeps a squadron, at immense cost, on the coast of Africa. Every-where, in this country, it is safe to speak of this foreign slave-trade, as a most inhuman traffic, opposed alike to the laws of God and of man. The duty to extirpate and destroy it, is admitted even by our *Doctors of Divinity*. In order to put an. end to it, some of these last have consented that their colored brethren (nominally free) should leave this country, and establish themselves on the western coast of Africa! It is, however, a notable fact, that, while so much execration is poured out by Americans, upon those engaged in the foreign slave-trade, the men engaged in the slave-trade between the states pass without condemnation, and their business is deemed honorable.

Behold the practical operation of this internal slave-trade, the American slave-trade, sustained by American politics and American religion. Here you will see men and women, reared like swine, for the market. You know what is a swine-drover? I will show you a man-drover. They inhabit all our Southern States. They perambulate the country, and crowd the highways of the nation, with droves of human stock. You will see one of these human flesh jobbers, armed with pistol, whip and bowie-knife, driving a company of a hundred men, women, and children, from the Potomac to the slave market at New Orleans. These wretched people are to be sold singly, or in lots, to suit purchasers. They are food for the cotton-field, and the deadly sugar-mill. Mark the sad procession, as it moves wearily along, and the inhuman wretch who drives them. Hear his savage yells and his blood-chilling oaths, as he hurries on his affrighted captives! There, see the old man, with locks thinned and gray. Cast one glance, if you please, upon that young mother, whose shoulders are bare to the scorching sun, her briny tears falling on the brow of the babe in her arms. See, too, that girl of thirteen, weeping, yes! weeping, as she thinks of the mother from whom she has been torn! The drove moves tardily. Heat and sorrow have nearly consumed their strength; suddenly you hear a quick snap, like the discharge of a rifle; the fetters clank, and the chain rattles simultaneously; your ears are saluted with a scream, that seems to have torn its way to the centre of your soul! The crack you heard, was the sound of the slave-whip; the scream you heard, was from the woman you saw with the babe. Her speed had faltered under the weight of her child and her chains! that gash on her shoulder tells her to move on. Follow this drove to New Orleans. Attend the auction; see men examined like horses; see the forms of women rudely and brutally exposed to the shocking gaze of American slave-buyers. See this drove sold and separated for ever; and never forget the deep, sad sobs that arose from that scattered multitude. Tell me citizens, *where*, under the sun, you can witness a spectacle more fiendish and shocking. Yet this is but a. glance at the American slave-trade, as it exists, at this moment, in the ruling part of the United States.

I was born amid such sights and scenes. To me the American slave-trade is a terrible reality. When a child, my soul was often pierced with a sense of its horrors. I lived on Philpot Street, Fell's Point, Baltimore, and have watched from the wharves, the slave ships in the Basin, anchored from the shore, with their cargoes of human flesh, waiting for favorable winds to waft them down the Chesapeake. There was, at that time, a grand slave mart kept at the head of Pratt Street, by

Austin Woldfolk. His agents were sent into every town and county in Maryland, announcing their arrival, through the papers, and on flaming "hand-bills," headed *cash for negroes.* These men were generally well dressed men, and very captivating in their manners. Ever ready to drink, to treat, and to gamble. The fate of many a slave has depended upon the turn of a single card; and many a child has been snatched from the arms of its mother, by bargains arranged in a state of brutal drunkenness.

The flesh-mongers gather up their victims by dozens, and drive them, chained, to the general depot at Baltimore. When a sufficient number have been collected here, a ship is chartered, for the purpose of conveying the forlorn crew to Mobile, or to New Orleans. From the slave prison to the ship, they are usually driven in the darkness of night; for since the anti-slavery agitation, a certain caution is observed.

In the deep still darkness of midnight, I have been often aroused by the dead heavy footsteps, and the pitious cries of the chained gangs that passed our door. The anguish of my boyish heart was intense; and I was often consoled, when speaking to my mistress in the morning, to hear her say that the custom was very wicked; that she hated to hear the rattle of the chains, and the heart-rending cries. I was glad to find one who sympathised with me in my horror.

Fellow-citizens, this murderous traffic is, to-day, in active operation in this boasted republic. In the solitude of my spirit, I see clouds of dust raised on the highways of the South; I see the bleeding footsteps; I hear the doleful wail of fettered humanity, on the way to the slave-markets, where the victims are to be sold like horses, sheep, and swine, knocked off to the highest bidder. There I see the tenderest ties ruthlessly broken, to gratify the lust, caprice and rapacity of the buyers and sellers of men. My soul sickens at the sight.

"Is this the land your Fathers loved, The freedom which they toiled to win? Is this the earth whereon they moved? Are these the graves they slumber in?"

But a still more inhuman, disgraceful, and scandalous state of things remains to be presented.

By an act of the American Congress, not yet two years old, slavery has been nationalized in its most horrible and revolting form. By that act, Mason & Dixon's line has been obliterated; New York has become as Virginia; and the power to hold, hunt, and sell men, women and childreH, as slaves, remains no longer a mere state institution, but is now an institution of the whole United States. The power is co-extensive with the star-spangled banner, and American Christianity. Where these go, may also go the merciless slave-hunter. Where these are, man is not sacred. He is a bird for the sportsman's gun./ By that most foul and fiendish of all human decrees, the liberty and person of every man are put in peril. Your broad republican domain is hunting ground for men. Not for thieves and robbers, enemies of society, merely, but for men guilty of no crime. Your law-makers have commanded all good citizens to engage in this hellish sport. Your President, your Secretary of State, your lords, nobles, and ecclesiastics, enforce, as a duty you owe to your free and glorious country, and to your God, that you do this accursed thing. Not fewer than forty Americans, have, within the past two years, been hunted down, and, without a moment's warning, hurried away in chains, and consigned to slavery, and excruciating torture. Some of these have had wives and children, dependent on them for bread; but of this, no account was made. The right of the hunter to his prey, stands superior to the right of marriage, and to all rights in this republic, the rights of God included! For black men there are neither law, justice, humanity, nor religion.

The Fugitive Slave Law makes *Mercy to Them, a Crime*; and bribes the judge who tries them. An American *Judge gets ten dollars for every victim he consigns* to slavery, and five, when he fails to do so. The oath of any two villains is sufficient, under this hell-black enactment, to send the most pious and exemplary black man into the remorseless jaws of slavery! His own testimony is nothing. He can bring no witnesses for himself. The minister of American justice is bound, by the law to hear but one side; and that side, is the side of the oppressor. Let this damning fact be perpetually told. Let it be thundered around the world, that, in tyrant-killing, king-hating, people-loving, democratic, Christian America, the seats of justice are filled with judges, who hold their offices under an open and palpable bribes, and are bound, in deciding in the case of a man's liberty, to hear only his accusers!

In glaring violation of justice, in shameless disregard of the forms of administering law, in cunning arrangement to entrap the defenceless, and in diabolical intent, this Fugitive Slave Law stands alone in the annals of tyrannical legislation. I doubt if there be another nation on the globe, having the brass and the baseness to put such a law on the statute-book. If any man in this assembly thinks differently from me in this matter, and feels able to disprove my statements, I will gladly confront him at any suitable time and place he may select.

Religious Liberty

I take this law to be one of the grossest infringements of Christian Liberty, and, if the churches and ministers of our country were not stupidly blind, or most wickedly indifferent, they, too, would so regard it.

At the very moment that they are thanking God for the enjoyment of civil and religious liberty, and for the right to worship God according to the dictates of their own consciences, they are utterly silent in respect to a law which robs religion of its chief significance, and makes it utterly worthless to a world lying in wickedness. Did this law concern the "mint, anise and cummin,"—abridge the right to sing psalms, to partake of the sacrament, or to engage in any of the ceremonies of religion, it would be smitten by the thunder of a thousand pulpits. A general shout would go up from the church, demanding repeal, repeal, instant repeal!—And it would go hard with that politician who presumed to solicit the votes of the people without inscribing this motto on his banner. Further, if this demand were not complied with, another Scotland would be added to the history of religious liberty, and the stern old covenanters would be thrown into the shade. A John Knox would be seen at every church door, and heard from every pulpit, and Fillmore would have no more quarter than was shown by Knox, to the beautiful, but treacherous Queen Mary of Scotland.—The fact that the church of our country, (with fractional exceptions,) does not esteem "the Fugitive Slave Law" as a declaration of war against religious liberty, implies that that church regards religion simply as a form of worship, an empty ceremony, and not a vital principle, requiring active benevolence, justice, love and good will towards man. It esteems sacrifice above mercy; psalm-singing above right doing; solemn meetings above practical righteousness. A worship that can be conducted by persons who refuse to give shelter to the houseless, to give bread to the hungry, clothing to the naked, and who enjoin obedience to a law forbidding these acts of mercy, is a curse, not a blessing to mankind. The Bible addresses all such persons as "scribes, pharisees, hypocrites, who pay tithe of mint, anise, and cummin, and have omitted the weightier matters of the law, judgment, mercy and faith."

The Church Responsible

But the church of this country is not only indifferent to the wrongs of the slave, it actually takes sides with the oppressors. It has made itself the bulwark of American slavery, and the shield of American slave-hunters. Many of its most eloquent Divines, who stand as the very lights of the church, have shamelessly given the sanction of religion, and the bible, to the whole slave system. — They have taught that man may, properly, be a slave; that the relation of master and slave is ordained of God; that to send back an escaped bondman to his master is clearly the duty of all the followers of the Lord Jesus Christ; and this horrible blasphemy is palmed off upon the world for christianity.

For my part, I would say, welcome infidelity! welcome atheism! welcome anything! in preference to the gospel, as p r eached by those Divines! They convert the very name of religion into an engine of tyranny, and barbarous cruelty, and serve to confirm more infidels, in this age, than all the infidel writings of Thomas Paine, Voltaire, and Bolingbroke, put together, have done? These ministers make religion a cold and flinty-hearted thing, having neither principles of right action, nor bowels of compassion. They strip the love of God of its beauty, and leave the throne of religion a huge, horrible, repulsive form. It is a religion for oppressors, tyrants, man-stealers, and thugs. It is not that "pare and undefiled religion" which is from above, and which is "first pure, then peaceable, easy to be entreated, full of mercy and good fruits, without partiality, and without hypocrisy." But a religion which favors the rich against the poor; which exalts the proud above the humble; which divides mankind into two classes, tyrants and slaves; which says to the man in chains, stay there; and to the oppressor, oppress on; it is a religion which may be professed and enjoyed by all the robbers and enslavers of mankind; it makes God a respecter of persons, denies his fatherhood of the race, and tramples in the dust the great truth of the brotherhood of man. All this we affirm to be true of the popular church, and the popular worship of our land and nation—a religion, a church and a worship which, on the authority of inspired wisdom, we pronounce to be an abomination in the sight of God. In the language of Isaiah, the American church might be well addressed, "Bring no more vain oblations; incense is an abomination unto me : the new moons and Sabbaths, the calling of assemblies, I cannot away with it is iniquity, even the solemn meeting. Your new moons, and your appointed feasts my soul hatest. They are a trouble to me; I am weary to bear them; and when ye spread forth your hands I will hide mine eyes from you. Yea! when ye make many prayers, I will not hear. *Your hands are full of blood*; cease to do evil, learn to do well; seek judgment; relieve the oppressed; judge for the fatherless; plead for the widow."

The American church is guilty, when viewed in connection with what it is doing to uphold slavery; but it is superlatively guilty when viewed in connection with its ability to abolish slavery.

The sin of which it is guilty is one of omission as well as of commission. Albert Barnes but uttered what the common sense of every man at all observant of the actual state of the case will receive as truth, when he declared that "There is no power out of the church that could sustain slavery an hour, if it were not sustained in it."

Let the religious press, the pulpit, the sunday school, the conference meeting, the great ecclesiastical, missionary, bible and tract associations of the land array their immense powers against slavery, and slave-holding; and the whole system of crime and blood would be scattered to the winds, and that they do not do this involves them in the most awful responsibility of which the mind can conceive.

In prosecuting the anti-slavery enterprise, we have been asked to spare the church, to spare the ministry; but how, we ask, could such a thing be done? We are met on the threshold of our efforts for the redemption of the slave, by the church. and ministry of the country, in battle arrayed against us; and we are compelled to fight or flee. From what quarter, I beg to know, has proceeded a fire so deadly upon our ranks, during the last two years, as from the Northern pulpit? As the champions of oppressors, the chosen men of American theology have appeared—men, honored for their so called piety, and their real learning. The *Lords* of Buffalo, the *Springs* of New York, the *Lathrops* of Auburn, the *Coxes* and *Spencers* of Brooklyn, the *Gannets* and *Sharps* of Boston, the *Deweys* of Washington, and other great religious lights of the land, have, in utter denial of the authority of Him, by whom they professed to be called to the ministry, deliberately taught us, against the example of the Hebrews, and against the remonstrance of the Apostles, they teach that we ought to obey man's law before the law of God."

My spirit wearies of such blasphemy; and how such men can be supported, as the "standing types and representatives of Jesus Christ," is a mystery which I leave others to penetrate. In speaking of the American church, however, let it be distinctly understood that I mean the great mass of the religious organizations of our land. There are exceptions, and I thank God that there are. Noble men may be found, scattered all over these Northern States, of whom Henry Ward Beecher, of Brooklyn, Samuel J. May, of Syracuse, and my esteemed friend* on the platform, are shining examples; and let me say further, that, upon these men lies the duty to inspire our ranks with high religious faith and zeal, and to cheer us on in the great mission of the slave's redemption from his chains.

Religion in England and Religion in America

One is struck with the difference between the attitude of the American church towards the anti-slavery movement, and that occupied by the churches in England towards a similar movement in that country. There, the church, true to its mission of ameliorating, elevating, and improving the condition of mankind, came forward promptly, bound up the wounds of the West Indian slave, and restored him to his liberty. There, the question of emancipation was a high religious question. It was demanded, in the name of humanity, and according to the law of the living God. The Sharps, the Clarksons, the Wilberforces, the Buxtons, the Burchells and the Knibbs, were alike famous for their piety, and for their philanthropy. The anti-slavery movement there, was not an anti-church movement, for the reason that the church took its full share in prosecuting that movement : and the anti-slavery movement in this country will cease to be an anti-church movement, when the church of this country shall assume a favorable, instead of a hostile position towards that movement.

Americans! your republican politics, not less than your republican religion, are flagrantly inconsistent. You boast of your love of liberty, your superior civilization, and your pure christianity, while the whole political power of the nation, (as embodied in the two great political parties, is solemnly pledged to support and perpetuate the enslavement of three millions of your countrymen. You hurl your anathemas at the crowned headed tyrants of Russia and Austria, and pride yourselves on your Democratic institutions, while you yourselves consent to be the mere tools and body-guards of the tyrants of Virginia and Carolina. You invite to your shores fugitives of oppression from abroad, honor them with banquets, greet them with ovations, cheer them, toast them, salute them, protect them, and pour out your money to them like water; but the fugitives from your own land, you advertise, hunt, arrest, shoot and kill.

You glory in your refinement, and your universal education; yet you maintain a system as barbarous and dreadful, as ever stained the character of a nation—a system begun in avarice, supported in pride, and perpetuated in cruelty. You shed tears over fallen Hungary, and make the sad story of her wrongs the theme of your poets, statesmen and orators, till your gallant sons are ready to fly to arms to vindicate her cause against her oppressors; but, in regard to the ten thousand wrongs of the American slave, you would enforce the strictest silence, and would hail him as an enemy of the nation who dares to make those wrongs the subject of public discourse! You are all on fire at the mention of liberty for France or for Ireland; but are as cold as an iceberg at the thought of liberty for the enslaved of America.—You discourse eloquently on the dignity of labor; yet, you sustain a system which, in its very essence, casts a stigma upon labor. You can bare your bosom to the storm of British artillery, to throw off a three-penny tax on tea; and yet wring the last hard earned farthing from the grasp of the black laborers of your country. You profess to believe "that, of one blood, God made all nations of men to dwell on the face of all the earth," and hath commanded all men, everywhere to love one another; yet you notoriously hate, (and glory in your hatred,) all men whose skins are not colored like your own. You declare, before the world, and are understood by the world to declare, that you "hold these truths to be self evident, that all men are created equal; and are endowed by their Creator with certain, inalienable rights; and that, among these are, life, liberty, and the pursuit of happiness; and yet, you hold securely, in a bondage, which according to your own Thomas Jefferson, "is worse than ages of that which your fathers rose in rebellion to oppose," a seventh part of the inhabitants of your country.

Fellow-citizens! I will not enlarge further on your national inconsistencies. The existence of slavery in this country brands your republicanism as a sham, your humanity as a base pretence, and your christianity as a lie. It destroys your moral power abroad it corrupts your politicians at home. It saps the foundation of religion; it makes your name a hissing, and a bye-word to a mocking earth. It is the antagonistic force in your government, the only thing that seriously disturbs and endangers your Union. It fetters your progress; it is the enemy of improvement, the deadly foe of education; it fosters pride; it breeds insolence; it promotes vice; it shelters crime; it is a curse to the earth that supports it; and yet, you cling to it, as if it were the sheet anchor of all your hopes. Oh! be warned! be warned! a horrible reptile is coiled up in your nation's bosom; the venomous creature is nursing at the tender breast of your youthful republic; for the love of God, tear away, and fling from you the hideous monster, and let the weight of twenty millions, crush and destroy it forever!

The Constitution

But it is answered in reply to all this, that precisely what I have now denounced is, in fact, guaranteed and sanctioned by the Constitution of the United States; that, the right to hold, and to hunt slaves is a part of that Constitution framed by the illustrious Fathers of this Republic.

Then, I dare to affirm, notwithstanding all I have said before, your fathers stooped, basely stooped.

"To palter with us in a double sense : And keep the word of promise to the ear, But break it to the heart."

And instead of being the honest men I have before declared them to be, they were the veriest imposters that ever practised on mankind. This is the inevitable conclusion, and from it there is no escape; but I differ from those who charge this baseness on the framers of the Constitution of the United States. It is a slander upon their memory, at least, so I believe. There is not time now to argue the constitutional question at length; nor have I the ability to discuss it as it ought to be discussed. The subject has been handled with masterly power by Lysander Spooner, Esq., by William Goodell, by Samuel E. Sewall, Esq., and last, though not least, by Gerritt Smith, Esq. These gentlemen have, as I think, fully and clearly vindicated the Constitution from any design to support slavery for an hour.

Fellow-citizens! there is no matter in respect to which, the people of the North have allowed themselves to be so ruinously imposed upon, as that of the pro-slavery character of the Constitution. In that instrument I hold there is neither warrant, license, nor sanction of the hateful thing; but interpreted, as it ought to be interpreted, the Constitution is a *Glorious Liberty Document*. Read its preamble, consider its purposes. Is slavery among them? Is it at the gateway? or is it in the temple? it is neither. While I do not intend to argue this question on the present occasion, let me ask, if it be not somewhat singular that, if the Constitution were intended to be, by its framers and adopters, a slave-holding instrument, why neither slavery, slaveholding, nor slave can anywhere be found in it. What would be thought of an instrument, drawn up, legally drawn up, for the purpose of entitling the city of Rochester to a track of land, in which no mention of land was made? Now, there are certain rules of interpretation, for the proper understanding of all legal instruments. These rules are well established. They are plain, common-sense rules, such as you and I, and all of us, can understand and apply, without having passed years in the study of law. I scout the idea that the question of the constitutionality, or un. constitutionality of slavery, is not a question for the people. I hold that every American citizen has a right to form an opinion of the constitution, and to propagate that opinion, and to use all honorable means to make his opinion the prevailing one. With out this right, the liberty of an American citizen would be as insecure as that of a Frenchman. Ex-Vice-President Dallas tells us that the constitution is an object to which no American mind can be too attentive, and no American heart too devoted. He further says, the constitution, in its words, is plain and intelligible, and is meant for the home-bred, unsophisticated understandings of our fellow-citizens. Senator Berrien tells us that the Constitution is the fundamental law, that which controls all others. The charter of our liberties, which every citizen has a personal interest in understanding thoroughly. The testimony of Senator Breese, Lewis Cass, and many others that might be named, who are everywhere esteemed as sound lawyers, so regard the constitution. I take it, therefore, that it is not presumption in a private citizen to form an opinion of that instrument.

Now, take the constitution according to its plain reading, and I defy the presentation of a single pro . slavery clause in it. On the other hand it will be found to contain principles and purposes, entirely hostile to the existence of slavery.

I have detained my audience entirely too long already. At some future period I will gladly avail myself of an opportunity to give this subject a full and fair discussion.

Allow me to say, in conclusion, notwithstanding the dark picture I have this day presented, of the state of the nation, I do not despair of this country. There are forces in operation, which must inevitably, work the downfall of slavery. "The arm of the Lord is not shortened," and the doom of slavery is certain.

I, therefore, leave off where I began, with hope. While drawing encouragement from "the Declaration of Independence," the great principles it contains, and the genius of American Institutions, my spirit is also cheered by the obvious tendencies of the age. Nations do not now stand in the same relation to each other that they did ages ago. No nation can now shut itself up, from the surrounding world, and trot round in the same old path of its fathers without interference. The time was when such could be done. Long established customs of hurtful character could formerly fence themselves in, and do their evil work with social impunity. Knowledge was then confined and enjoyed by the privileged few, and the multitude walked on in mental darkness. But a change has now come over the affairs of mankind. Walled cities and empires have become unfashionable. The arm of commerce has borne away the gates of the strong city. Intelligence is penetrating the darkest corners of the globe. It makes its pathway over and under the sea, as well as on the earth. Wind, steam, and lightning are its chartered agents. Oceans no longer divide, but link nations together. From Boston to London is now a holiday excursion. Space is comparatively annihilated.—Thoughts expressed on one side of the Atlantic, are distinctly heard on the other.

The far off and almost fabulous Pacific rolls in grandeur at our feet. The Celestial Empire, the mystery of ages, is being solved. The fiat of the Almighty, "Let there be Light," has not yet spent its force. No abuse, no outrage whether in taste, sport or avarice, can now hide itself from the all-pervading light. The iron shoe, and crippled foot of China must be seen, in contrast with nature. Afric must rise and put on her yet unwoven garment. "Ethiopia shall stretch out her hand unto God." In the fervent aspirations of William Lloyd Garrison, I say, and let every heart join in saying it :

God speed the year of jubilee
The wide world o'er!
When from their galling chains set free,
Th' oppress'd shall vilely bend the knee,
And wear the yoke of tyranny
Like brutes no more.
That year will come, and freedom's reign,
To man his plundered rights again Restore.
God speed the day when human blood
Shall cease to flow!
In every clime be understood,
The claims of human brotherhood,
And each return for evil, good,
Not blow for _blow;
That day will come all feuds to end,
And change into a faithful friend
Each foe.
God speed the hour, the glorious hour,
When none on earth
Shall exercise a lordly power,
Nor in a tyrant's presence cower;
But all to manhood's stature tower,
By equal birth!
That Hour Will Come, to each, to all,
And from his prison-house, the thrall Go forth.
Until that year, day, hour, arrive,
With head, and heart, and hand I'll strive,
To break the rod, and rend the gyve,
The spoiler of his prey deprive
So witness Heaven!
And never from my chosen post,
Whate'er the peril or the cost,
Be driven.

What the Black Man Wants

Delivered to The Massachusetts Anti-Slavery Society at Boston

Mr. President, I came here, as I come always to the meetings in New England, as a listener, and not as a speaker; and one of the reasons why I have not been more frequently to the meetings of this society, has been because of the disposition on the part of some of my friends to call me out upon the platform, even when they knew that there was some difference of opinion and of feeling between those who rightfully belong to this platform and myself; and for fear of being misconstrued, as desiring to interrupt or disturb the proceedings of these meetings, I have usually kept away, and have thus been deprived of that educating influence, which I am always free to confess is of the highest order, descending from this platform. I have felt, since I have lived out West, that in going there I parted from a great deal that was valuable; and I feel, every time I come to these meetings, that I have lost a great deal by making my home west of Boston, west of Massachusetts; for, if anywhere in the country there is to be found the highest sense of justice, or the truest demands for my race, I look for it in the East, I look for it here. The ablest discussions of the whole question of our rights occur here, and to be deprived of the privilege of listening to those discussions is a great deprivation.

I do not know, from what has been said, that there is any difference of opinion as to the duty of abolitionists, at the present moment. How can we get up any difference at this point, or at any point, where we are so united, so agreed? I went especially, however, with that word of Mr. Phillips, which is the criticism of Gen. Banks and Gen. Banks's policy. I hold that that policy is our chief danger at the present moment; that it practically enslaves the negro, and makes the Proclamation of 1863 a mockery and delusion. What is freedom? It is the right to choose one's own employment. Certainly it means that, if it means any thing; and when any individual or combination of individuals, undertakes to decide for any man when he shall work, where he shall work, at what he shall work, and for what he shall work, he or they practically reduce him to slavery. (Applause.) He is a slave. That I understand Gen. Banks to do — to determine for the so-called freedman, when, and where, and at what, and for how much he shall work, when he shall be punished, and by whom punished. It is absolute slavery. It defeats the beneficent intentions of the Government, if it has beneficent intentions, in regard to the freedom of our people.

I have had but one idea for the last three years, to present to the American people, and the phraseology in which I clothe it is the old abolition phraseology. I am for the "immediate, unconditional, and universal" enfranchisement of the black man, in every State in the Union. (Loud applause.) Without this, his liberty is a mockery; without this, you might as well almost retain the old name of slavery for his condition; for, in fact, if he is not the slave of the individual master, he is the slave of society, and holds his liberty as a privilege, not as a right. He is at the mercy of the mob, and has no means of protecting himself.

It may be objected, however, that this pressing of the negro's right to suffrage is premature. Let us have slavery abolished, it may be said, let us have labor organized, and then, in the natural course of events, the right of suffrage will be extended to the negro. I do not agree with this. The constitution of the human mind is such, that if it once disregards the conviction forced upon it by a revelation of truth, it requires the exercise of a higher power to produce the same conviction afterwards. The American people are now in tears. The Shenandoah has run blood — the best blood of the North. All around Richmond, the blood of New England and of the North has been shed — of your sons, your brothers and your fathers. We all feel, in the existence of this Rebellion, that judgments terrible, wide-spread, far-reaching, overwhelming, are abroad in the land; and we feel, in view of these judgments, just now, a disposition to learn righteousness. This is the hour. Our streets are in mourning, tears are falling at every fireside, and under the chastisement of this Rebellion we have almost come up to the point of conceding this great, this all-important right of suffrage. I fear that if we fail to do it now, if abolitionists fail to press it now, we may not see, for centuries to come, the same disposition that exists at this moment. (Applause.) Hence, I say, now is the time to press this right.

It may be asked, "Why do you want it? Some men have got along very well without it. Women have not this right." Shall we justify one wrong by another? That is a sufficient answer. Shall we at this moment justify the deprivation of the negro of the right to vote, because some one else is deprived of that privilege? I hold that women, as well as men, have the right to vote (applause), and my heart, and my voice go with the movement to extend suffrage to woman; but that question rests upon another basis than that on which our right rests. We may be asked, I say, why we want it. I will tell you why we want it. We want it because it is our right, first of all. (Applause.) No class of men can, without insulting their own nature, be content with any deprivation of their rights. We want it, again, as a means for educating our race. Men are so constituted that they derive their conviction of their own possibilities largely from the estimate formed of them by others. If nothing is expected of a people, that people will find it difficult to contradict that expectation. By depriving us of suffrage, you affirm our incapacity to form an intelligent judgment respecting public men and public measures; you declare before the world that we are unfit to exercise the elective franchise, and by this means lead us to undervalue ourselves, to put a low estimate upon ourselves, and to feel that we have no possibilities like other men. Again, I want the elective franchise, for one, as a colored man, because ours is a peculiar government, based upon a peculiar idea, and that idea is universal suffrage. If I were in a monarchical government, or an autocratic or aristocratic government, where the few bore rule and the many were subject, there would be no special stigma resting upon me, because I did not exercise the elective franchise. It would do me no great violence. Mingling with the mass, I should partake of the strength of the mass; I should be supported by the mass, and I should have the same incentives to endeavor with the mass of my fellow-men; it would be no particular burden, no particular deprivation; but here, where universal suffrage is the rule, where that is the fundamental idea of the Government, to rule us out is to make us an exception, to brand us with the stigma of inferiority, and to invite to our heads the missiles of those about us; therefore, I want the franchise for the black man.

There are, however, other reasons, not derived from any consideration merely of our rights, but arising out of the condition of the South, and of the country - considerations which have already been referred to by Mr. Phillips - considerations which must arrest the attention of statesmen. I believe that when the tall heads of this Rebellion shall have been swept down, as they will be swept down, when the Davises and Toombses and Stephenses, and others who are leading in this Rebellion shall have been blotted out, there will be this rank undergrowth of treason, to which reference has been made, growing up there, and interfering with, and thwarting the quiet operation of the Federal Government in those States. You will see those traitors handing down, from sire to son, the same malignant spirit which they have manifested, and which they are now exhibiting, with malicious hearts, broad blades, and bloody hands in the field, against our sons and brothers. That spirit will still remain; and whoever sees the Federal Government extended over those Southern States will see that Government in a strange land, and not only in a strange land, but in an enemy's land. A post-master of the United States in the South will find himself surrounded by a hostile spirit; a collector in a Southern port will find himself surrounded by a hostile spirit; a United States marshal or United States judge will be surrounded there by a hostile element. That enmity will not die out in a year, will not die out in an age. The Federal Government will be looked upon in those States precisely as the Governments of Austria and France are looked upon in Italy at the present moment. They will endeavor to circumvent, they will endeavor to destroy, the peaceful operation of this Government. Now, where will you find the strength to counterbalance this spirit, if you do not find it in the negroes of the South? They are your friends, and have always been your friends. They were your friends even when the Government did not regard them as such. They comprehended the genius of this war before you did. It is a significant fact, it is a marvellous fact, it seems almost to imply a direct interposition of Providence, that this war, which began in the interest of slavery on both sides, bids fair to end in the interest of liberty on both sides. (Applause.) It was begun, I say, in the interest of slavery on both sides. The South was fighting to take slavery out of the Union, and the North fighting to keep it in the Union; the South fighting to get it beyond the limits of the United-States Constitution, and the North fighting to retain it within those limits; the South fighting for new guarantees, and the North fighting for the old guarantees; — both despising the negro, both insulting the negro. Yet, the negro, apparently endowed with wisdom from on high, saw more clearly the end from the beginning than we did. When Seward said the status of no man in the country would be changed by the war, the negro did not believe him. (Applause.) When our generals sent their underlings in shoulder-straps to hunt the flying negro back from our lines into the jaws of slavery, from which he had escaped, the negroes thought that a mistake had been made, and that the intentions of the Government had not been rightly understood by our officers in shoulder-straps, and they continued to come into our lines, threading their way through bogs and fens, over briers and thorns, fording streams, swimming rivers, bringing us tidings as to the safe path to march, and pointing out the dangers that threatened us. They are our only friends in the South, and we should be true to them in this their trial hour, and see to it that they have the elective franchise.

I know that we are inferior to you in some things — virtually inferior. We walk about among you like dwarfs among giants. Our heads are scarcely seen above the great sea of humanity. The Germans are superior to us; the Irish are superior to us; the Yankees are superior to us (laughter); they can do what we cannot, that is, what we have not hitherto been allowed to do. But while I make this admission, I utterly deny that we are originally, or naturally, or practically, or in any way, or in any important sense, inferior to anybody on this globe. (Loud applause.) This charge of inferiority is an old dodge. It has been made available for oppression on many occasions. It is only about six centuries since the blue-eyed and fair-haired Anglo-Saxons were considered inferior by the haughty Normans, who once trampled upon them. If you read the history of the Norman Conquest, you will find that this proud Anglo-Saxon was once looked upon as of coarser clay than his Norman master, and might be found in the highways and byways of old England laboring with a brass collar on his neck, and the name of his master marked upon it. You were down then! (Laughter and applause.) You are up now. I am glad you are up, and I want you to be glad to help us up also. (Applause.)

The story of our inferiority is an old dodge, as I have said; for wherever men oppress their fellows, wherever they enslave them, they will endeavor to find the needed apology for such enslavement and oppression in the character of the people oppressed and enslaved. When we wanted, a few years ago, a slice of Mexico, it was hinted that the Mexicans were an inferior race, that the old Castilian blood had become so weak that it would scarcely run down hill, and that Mexico needed the long, strong and beneficent arm of the Anglo-Saxon care extended over it. We said that it was necessary to its salvation, and a part of the "manifest destiny" of this Republic, to extend our arm over that dilapidated government. So, too, when Russia wanted to take possession of a part of the Ottoman Empire, the Turks were "an inferior race." So, too, when England wants to set the heel of her power more firmly in the quivering heart of old Ireland, the Celts are an "inferior race." So, too, the negro, when he is to be robbed of any right which is justly his, is an "inferior man." It is said that we are ignorant; I admit it. But if we know enough to be hung, we know enough to vote. If the negro knows enough to pay taxes to support the government, he knows enough to vote; taxation and representation should go together. If he knows enough to shoulder a musket and fight for the flag, fight for the government, he knows enough to vote. If he knows as much when he is sober as an Irishman knows when drunk, he knows enough to vote, on good American principles. (Laughter and applause.)

But I was saying that you needed a counterpoise in the persons of the slaves to the enmity that would exist at the South after the Rebellion is put down. I hold that the American people are bound, not only in self-defence, to extend this right to the freedmen of the South, but they are bound by their love of country, and by all their regard for the future safety of those Southern States, to do this — to do it as a measure essential to the preservation of peace there. But I will not dwell upon this. I put it to the American sense of honor. The honor of a nation is an important thing. It is said in the Scriptures, "What doth it profit a man if he gain the whole world, and lose his own soul?" It may be said, also, What doth it profit a nation if it gain the whole world, but lose its honor? I hold that the American government has taken upon itself a solemn obligation of honor, to see that this war — let it be long or let it be short, let it cost much or let it cost little — that this war shall not cease until every freedman at the South has the right to vote. (Applause.) It has bound itself to it. What have you asked the black men of the South, the black men of the whole country, to do? Why, you have asked them to incur the deadly enmity of their masters, in order to befriend you and to befriend this Government. You have asked us to call down, not only upon ourselves, but upon our children's children, the deadly hate of the entire Southern people. You have called upon us to turn our backs upon our masters, to abandon their cause and espouse yours; to turn against the South and in favor of the North; to shoot down the Confederacy and uphold the flag — the American flag. You have called upon us to expose ourselves to all the subtle machinations of their malignity for all time. And now, what do you propose to do when you come to make peace? To reward your enemies, and trample in the dust your friends? Do you intend to sacrifice the very men who have come to the rescue of your banner in the South, and incurred the lasting displeasure of their masters thereby? Do you intend to sacrifice them and reward your enemies? Do you mean to give your enemies the right to vote, and take it away from your friends? Is that wise policy? Is that honorable? Could American honor withstand such a blow? I do not believe you will do it. I think you will see to it that we have the right to vote. There is something too mean in looking upon the negro, when you are in trouble, as a citizen, and when you are free from trouble, as an alien. When this nation was in trouble, in its early struggles, it looked upon the negro as a citizen. In 1776 he was a citizen. At the time of the formation of the Constitution the negro had the right to vote in eleven States out of the old thirteen. In your trouble you have made us citizens. In 1812 Gen. Jackson addressed us as citizens — "fellow-citizens." He wanted us to fight. We were citizens then! And now, when you come to frame a conscription bill, the negro is a citizen again. He has been a citizen just three times in the history of this government, and it has always been in time of trouble. In time of trouble we are citizens. Shall we be citizens in war, and aliens in peace? Would that be just?

I ask my friends who are apologizing for not insisting upon this right, where can the black man look, in this country, for the assertion of this right, if he may not look to the Massachusetts Anti-Slavery Society? Where under the whole heavens can he look for sympathy, in asserting this right, if he may not look to this platform? Have you lifted us up to a certain height to see that we are men, and then are any disposed to leave us there, without seeing that we are put in possession of all our rights? We look naturally to this platform for the assertion of all our rights, and for this one especially. I understand the anti-slavery societies of this country to be based on two principles, — first, the freedom of the blacks of this country; and, second, the elevation of them. Let me not be misunderstood here. I am not asking for sympathy at the hands of abolitionists, sympathy at the hands of any. I think the American people are disposed often to be generous rather than just. I look over this country at the present time, and I see Educational Societies, Sanitary Commissions, Freedmen's Associations, and the like, — all very good: but in regard to the colored people there is always more that is benevolent, I perceive, than just, manifested towards us. What I ask for the negro is not benevolence, not pity, not sympathy, but simply justice. (Applause.) The American people have always been anxious to know what they shall do with us. Gen. Banks was distressed with solicitude as to what he should do with the negro. Everybody has asked the question, and they learned to ask it early of the abolitionists, "What shall we do with the negro?" I have had but one answer from the beginning. Do nothing with us! Your doing with us has already played the mischief with us. Do nothing with us! If the apples will not remain on the tree of their own strength, if they are worm-eaten at the core, if they are early ripe and disposed to fall, let them fall! I am not for tying or fastening them on the tree in any way, except by nature's plan, and if they will not stay there, let them fall. And if the negro cannot stand on his own legs, let him fall also. All I ask is, give him a chance to stand on his own legs! Let him alone! If you see him on his way to school, let him alone, — don't disturb him! If you see him going to the dinner-table at a hotel, let him go! If you see him going to the ballot-box, let him alone, — don't disturb him! (Applause.) If you see him going into a work-shop, just let him alone, — your interference is doing him a positive injury. Gen. Banks's "preparation" is of a piece with this attempt to prop up the negro. Let him fall if he cannot stand alone! If the negro cannot live by the line of eternal justice, so beautifully pictured to you in the illustration used by Mr. Phillips, the fault will not be yours, it will be his who made the negro, and established that line for his government. (Applause.) Let him live or die by that. If you will only untie his hands, and give him a chance, I think he will live. He will work as readily for himself as the white man. A great many delusions have been swept away by this war. One was, that the negro would not work; he has proved his ability to work. Another was, that the negro would not fight; that he possessed only the most sheepish attributes of humanity; was a perfect lamb, or an "Uncle Tom;" disposed to take off his coat whenever required, fold his hands, and be whipped by anybody who wanted to whip him. But the war has proved that there is a great deal of human nature in the negro, and that "he will fight," as Mr. Quincy, our President, said, in earlier days than these, "when there is a reasonable possibility of his whipping anybody." (Laughter and applause.)

Appeal to Congress for Impartial Suffrage

January, 1867

A very limited statement of the argument for impartial suffrage, and for including the negro in the body politic, would require more space than can be reasonably asked here. It is supported by reasons as broad as the nature of man, and as numerous as the wants of society. Man is the only government-making animal in the world. His right to a participation in the production and operation of government is an inference from his nature, as direct and self-evident as is his right to acquire property or education. It is no less a crime against the manhood of a man, to declare that he shall not share in the making and directing of the government under which he lives, than to say that he shall not acquire property and education. The fundamental and unanswerable argument in favor of the enfranchisement of the negro is found in the undisputed fact of his manhood. He is a man, and by every fact and argument by which any man can sustain his right to vote, the negro can sustain his right equally. It is plain that, if the right belongs to any, it belongs to all. The doctrine that some men have no rights that others are bound to respect, is a doctrine which we must banish as we have banished slavery, from which it emanated. If black men have no rights in the eyes of white men, of course the whites can have none in the eyes of the blacks. The result is a war of races, and the annihilation of all proper human relations.

But suffrage for the negro, while easily sustained upon abstract principles, demands consideration upon what are recognized as the urgent necessities of the case. It is a measure of relief,—a shield to break the force of a blow already descending with violence, and render it harmless. The work of destruction has already been set in motion all over the South. Peace to the country has literally meant war to the loyal men of the South, white and black; and negro suffrage is the measure to arrest and put an end to that dreadful strife.

Something then, not by way of argument, (for that has been done by Charles Sumner, Thaddeus Stevens, Wendell Phillips, Gerrit Smith, and other able men,) but rather of statement and appeal.

For better or for worse, (as in some of the old marriage ceremonies,) the negroes are evidently a permanent part of the American population. They are too numerous and useful to be colonized, and too enduring and self-perpetuating to disappear by natural causes. Here they are, four millions of them, and, for weal or for woe, here they must remain. Their history is parallel to that of the country; but while the history of the latter has been cheerful and bright with blessings, theirs has been heavy and dark with agonies and curses. What O'Connell said of the history of Ireland may with greater truth be said of the negro's. It may be "traced like a wounded man through a crowd, by the blood." Yet the negroes have marvellously survived all the exterminating forces of slavery, and have emerged at the end of two hundred and fifty years of bondage, not morose, misanthropic, and revengeful, but cheerful, hopeful, and forgiving. They now stand before Congress and the country, not complaining of the past, but simply asking for a better future. The spectacle of these dusky millions thus imploring, not demanding, is touching; and if American statesmen could be moved by a simple appeal to the nobler elements of human nature, if they had not fallen, seemingly, into the incurable habit of weighing and measuring every proposition of reform by some standard of profit and loss, doing wrong from choice, and right only from necessity or some urgent demand of human selfishness, it would be enough to plead for the negroes on the score of past services and sufferings. But no such appeal shall be relied on here. Hardships, services, sufferings, and sacrifices are all waived. It is true that they came to the relief of the country at the hour of its extremest need. It is true that, in many of the rebellious States, they were almost the only reliable friends the nation had throughout the whole tremendous war. It is true that, notwithstanding their alleged ignorance, they were wiser than their masters, and knew enough to be loyal, while those masters only knew enough to be rebels and traitors. It is true that they fought side by side in the loyal cause with our gallant and patriotic white soldiers, and that, but for their help,—divided as the loyal States were,—the Rebels might have succeeded in breaking up the Union, thereby entailing border wars and troubles of unknown duration and incalculable calamity. All this and more is true of these loyal negroes. Many daring exploits will be told to their credit. Impartial history will paint them as men who deserved well of their country. It will tell how they forded and swam rivers, with what consummate address they evaded the sharp-eyed Rebel pickets, how they toiled in the darkness of night through the tangled marshes of briers and thorns, barefooted and weary, running the risk of losing their lives, to warn our generals of Rebel schemes to surprise and destroy our loyal army. It will tell how these poor people, whose rights we still despised, behaved to our wounded soldiers, when found cold, hungry, and bleeding on the deserted battle-field; how they assisted our escaping prisoners from Andersonville, Belle Isle, Castle Thunder, and elsewhere, sharing with them their wretched crusts, and otherwise affording them aid and comfort; how they promptly responded to the trumpet call for their services, fighting against a foe that denied them the rights of civilized warfare, and for a government which was without the courage to assert those rights and avenge their violation in their behalf; with what gallantry they flung themselves upon Rebel fortifications, meeting death as fearlessly as any other troops in the service. But upon none of these things is reliance placed. These facts speak to the better dispositions of the human heart; but they seem of little weight with the opponents of impartial suffrage.

It is true that a strong plea for equal suffrage might be addressed to the national sense of honor. Something, too, might be said of national gratitude. A nation might well hesitate before the temptation to betray its allies. There is something immeasurably mean, to say nothing of the cruelty, in placing the loyal negroes of the South under the political power of their Rebel masters. To make peace with our enemies is all well enough; but to prefer our enemies and sacrifice our friends,—to exalt our enemies and cast down our friends,—to clothe our enemies, who sought the destruction of the government, with all political power, and leave our friends powerless in their hands,—is an act which need not be characterized here. We asked the negroes to espouse our cause, to be our friends, to fight for us, and against their masters; and now, after they have done all that we asked them to do,—helped us to conquer their masters, and thereby directed toward themselves the furious hate of the vanquished,—it is proposed in some quarters to turn them over to the political control of the common enemy of the government and of the negro. But of this let nothing be said in this place. Waiving humanity, national honor, the claims of gratitude, the precious satisfaction arising from deeds of charity and justice to the weak and defenceless,—the appeal for impartial suffrage addresses itself with great pertinency to the darkest, coldest, and flintiest side of the human heart, and would wring righteousness from the unfeeling calculations of human selfishness.

For in respect to this grand measure it is the good fortune of the negro that enlightened selfishness, not less than justice, fights on his side. National interest and national duty, if elsewhere separated, are firmly united here. The American people can, perhaps, afford to brave the censure of surrounding nations for the manifest injustice and meanness of excluding its faithful black soldiers from the ballot-box, but it cannot afford to allow the moral and mental energies of rapidly increasing millions to be consigned to hopeless degradation.

Strong as we are, we need the energy that slumbers in the black man's arm to make us stronger. We want no longer any heavy- footed, melancholy service from the negro. We want the cheerful activity of the quickened manhood of these sable millions. Nor can we afford to endure the moral blight which the existence of a degraded and hated class must necessarily inflict upon any people among whom such a class may exist. Exclude the negroes as a class from political rights,—teach them that the high and manly privilege of suffrage is to be enjoyed by white citizens only,— that they may bear the burdens of the state, but that they are to have no part in its direction or its honors,—and you at once deprive them of one of the main incentives to manly character and patriotic devotion to the interests of the government; in a word, you stamp them as a degraded caste,—you teach them to despise themselves, and all others to despise them. Men are so constituted that they largely derive their ideas of their abilities and their possibilities from the settled judgments of their fellow-men, and especially from such as they read in the institutions under which they live. If these bless them, they are blest indeed; but if these blast them, they are blasted indeed. Give the negro the elective franchise, and you give him at once a powerful motive for all noble exertion, and make him a man among men. A character is demanded of him, and here as elsewhere demand favors supply. It is nothing against this reasoning that all men who vote are not good men or good citizens. It is enough that the possession and exercise of the elective franchise is in itself an appeal to the nobler elements of manhood, and imposes education as essential to the safety of society.

To appreciate the full force of this argument, it must be observed, that disfranchisement in a republican government based upon the idea of human equality and universal suffrage, is a very different thing from disfranchisement in governments based upon the idea of the divine right of kings, or the entire subjugation of the masses. Masses of men can take care of themselves. Besides, the disabilities imposed upon all are necessarily without that bitter and stinging element of invidiousness which attaches to disfranchisement in a republic. What is common to all works no special sense of degradation to any. But in a country like ours, where men of all nations, kindred, and tongues are freely enfranchised, and allowed to vote, to say to the negro, You shall not vote, is to deal his manhood a staggering blow, and to burn into his soul a bitter and goading sense of wrong, or else work in him a stupid indifference to all the elements of a manly character. As a nation, we cannot afford to have amongst us either this indifference and stupidity, or that burning sense of wrong. These sable millions are too powerful to be allowed to remain either indifferent or discontented. Enfranchise them, and they become self-respecting and country-loving citizens. Disfranchise them, and the mark of Cain is set upon them less mercifully than upon the first murderer, for no man was to hurt him. But this mark of inferiority—all the more palpable because of a difference of color—not only dooms the negro to be a vagabond, but makes him the prey of insult and outrage everywhere. While nothing may be urged here as to the past services of the negro, it is quite within the line of this appeal to remind the nation of the possibility that a time may come when the services of the negro may be a second time required. History is said to repeat itself, and, if so, having wanted the negro once, we may want him again. Can that statesmanship be wise which would leave the negro good ground to hesitate, when the exigencies of the country required his prompt assistance? Can that be sound statesmanship which leaves millions of men in gloomy discontent, and possibly in a state of alienation in the day of national trouble? Was not the nation stronger when two hundred thousand sable soldiers were hurled against the Rebel fortifications, than it would have been without them? Arming the negro was an urgent military necessity three years ago,—are we sure that another quite as pressing may not await us? Casting aside all thought of justice and magnanimity, is it wise to impose upon the negro all the burdens involved in sustaining government against foes within and foes without, to make him equal sharer in all sacrifices for the public good, to tax him in peace and conscript him in war, and then coldly exclude him from the ballot-box?

Look across the sea. Is Ireland, in her present condition, fretful, discontented, compelled to support an establishment in which she does not believe, and which the vast majority of her people abhor, a source of power or of weakness to Great Britain? Is not Austria wise in removing all ground of complaint against her on the part of Hungary? And does not the Emperor of Russia act wisely, as well as generously, when he not only breaks up the bondage of the serf, but extends him all the advantages of Russian citizenship? Is the present movement in England in favor of manhood suffrage—for the purpose of bringing four millions of British subjects into full sympathy and co-operation with the British government—a wise and humane movement, or otherwise? Is the existence of a rebellious element in our borders—which New Orleans, Memphis, and Texas show to be only disarmed, but at heart as malignant as ever, only waiting for an opportunity to reassert itself with fire and sword—a reason for leaving four millions of the nation's truest friends with just cause of complaint against the Federal government? If the doctrine that taxation should go hand in hand with representation can be appealed to in behalf of recent traitors and rebels, may it not properly be asserted in behalf of a people who have ever been loyal and faithful to the government? The answers to these questions are too obvious to require statement. Disguise it as we may, we are still a divided nation. The Rebel States have still an anti-national policy. Massachusetts and South Carolina may draw tears from the eyes of our tender-hearted President by walking arm in arm into his Philadelphia Convention, but a citizen of Massachusetts is still an alien in the Palmetto State. There is that, all over the South, which frightens Yankee industry, capital, and skill from its borders. We have crushed the Rebellion, but not its hopes or its malign purposes. The South fought for perfect and permanent control over the Southern laborer. It was a war of the rich against the poor. They who waged it had no objection to the government, while they could use it as a means of confirming their power over the laborer. They fought the government, not because they hated the government as such, but because they found it, as they thought, in the way between them and their one grand purpose of rendering permanent and indestructible their authority and power over the Southern laborer. Though the battle is for the present lost, the hope of gaining this object still exists, and pervades the whole South with a feverish excitement. We have thus far only gained a Union without unity, marriage without love, victory without peace. The hope of gaining by politics what they lost by the sword, is the secret of all this

Southern unrest; and that hope must be extinguished before national ideas and objects can take full possession of the Southern mind. There is but one safe and constitutional way to banish that mischievous hope from the South, and that is by lifting the laborer beyond the unfriendly political designs of his former master. Give the negro the elective franchise, and you at once destroy the purely sectional policy, and wheel the Southern States into line with national interests and national objects. The last and shrewdest turn of Southern politics is a recognition of the necessity of getting into Congress immediately, and at any price. The South will comply with any conditions but suffrage for the negro. It will swallow all the unconstitutional test oaths, repeal all the ordinances of Secession, repudiate the Rebel debt, promise to pay the debt incurred in conquering its people, pass all the constitutional amendments, if only it can have the negro left under its political control. The proposition is as modest as that made on the mountain: "All these things will I give unto thee if thou wilt fall down and worship me."

But why are the Southerners so willing to make these sacrifices? The answer plainly is, they see in this policy the only hope of saving something of their old sectional peculiarities and power. Once firmly seated in Congress, their alliance with Northern Democrats re-established, their States restored to their former position inside the Union, they can easily find means of keeping the Federal government entirely too busy with other important matters to pay much attention to the local affairs of the Southern States. Under the potent shield of State Rights, the game would be in their own hands. Does any sane man doubt for a moment that the men who followed Jefferson Davis through the late terrible Rebellion, often marching barefooted and hungry, naked and penniless, and who now only profess an enforced loyalty, would plunge this country into a foreign war to-day, if they could thereby gain their coveted independence, and their still more coveted mastery over the negroes? Plainly enough, the peace not less than the prosperity of this country is involved in the great measure of impartial suffrage. King Cotton is deposed, but only deposed, and is ready to-day to reassert all his ancient pretensions upon the first favorable opportunity. Foreign countries abound with his agents. They are able, vigilant, devoted. The young men of the South burn with the desire to regain what they call the lost cause; the women are noisily malignant towards the Federal government. In fact, all the elements of treason and rebellion are there under the thinnest disguise which necessity can impose.

What, then, is the work before Congress? It is to save the people of the South from themselves, and the nation from detriment on their account. Congress must supplant the evident sectional tendencies of the South by national dispositions and tendencies. It must cause national ideas and objects to take the lead and control the politics of those States. It must cease to recognize the old slave-masters as the only competent persons to rule the South. In a word, it must enfranchise the negro, and by means of the loyal negroes and the loyal white men of the South build up a national party there, and in time bridge the chasm between North and South, so that our country may have a common liberty and a common civilization. The new wine must be put into new bottles. The lamb may not be trusted with the wolf. Loyalty is hardly safe with traitors.

Statesmen of America! beware what you do. The ploughshare of rebellion has gone through the land beam-deep. The soil is in readiness, and the seed-time has come. Nations, not less than individuals, reap as they sow. The dreadful calamities of the past few years came not by accident, nor unbidden, from the ground. You shudder to-day at the harvest of blood sown in the spring-time of the Republic by your patriot fathers. The principle of slavery, which they tolerated under the erroneous impression that it would soon die out, became at last the dominant principle and power at the South. It early mastered the Constitution, became superior to the Union, and enthroned itself above the law.

Freedom of speech and of the press it slowly but successfully banished from the South, dictated its own code of honor and manners to the nation, brandished the bludgeon and the bowie-knife over Congressional debate, sapped the foundations of loyalty, dried up the springs of patriotism, blotted out the testimonies of the fathers against oppression, padlocked the pulpit, expelled liberty from its literature, invented nonsensical theories about master-races and slave-races of men, and in due season produced a Rebellion fierce, foul, and bloody.

This evil principle again seeks admission into our body politic. It comes now in shape of a denial of political rights to four million loyal colored people. The South does not now ask for slavery. It only asks for a large degraded caste, which shall have no political rights. This ends the case. Statesmen, beware what you do. The destiny of unborn and unnumbered generations is in your hands. Will you repeat the mistake of your fathers, who sinned ignorantly? or will you profit by the blood-bought wisdom all round you, and forever expel every vestige of the old abomination from our national borders? As you members of the Thirty-ninth Congress decide, will the country be peaceful, united, and happy, or troubled, divided, and miserable.

The Color Line

1881

Few evils are less accessible to the force of reason, or more tenacious of life and power, than a long-standing prejudice. It is a moral disorder, which creates the conditions necessary to its own existence, and fortifies itself by refusing all contradiction. It paints a hateful picture according to its own diseased imagination, and distorts the features of the fancied original to suit the portrait. As those who believe in the visibility of ghosts can easily see them, so it is always easy to see repulsive qualities in those we despise and hate.

Prejudice of race has at some time in their history afflicted all nations. "I am more holy than thou" is the boast of races, as well as that of the Pharisee. Long after the Norman invasion and the decline of Norman power, long after the sturdy Saxon had shaken off the dust of his humiliation and was grandly asserting his great qualities in all directions, the descendants of the invaders continued to regard their Saxon brothers as made of coarser clay than themselves, and were not well pleased when one of the former subject race came between the sun and their nobility. Having seen the Saxon a menial, a hostler, and a common drudge, oppressed and dejected for centuries, it was easy to invest him with all sorts of odious peculiarities, and to deny him all manly predicates. Though eight hundred years have passed away since Norman power entered England, and the Saxon has for centuries been giving his learning, his literature, his language, and his laws to the world more successfully than any other people on the globe, men in that country still boast their Norman origin and Norman perfections. This superstition of former greatness serves to fill out the shriveled sides of a meaningless race-pride which holds over after its power has vanished. With a very different lesson from the one this paper is designed to impress, the great Daniel Webster once told the people of Massachusetts (whose prejudices in the particular instance referred to were right) that they "had conquered the sea, and had conquered the land," but that "it remained for them to conquer their prejudices." At one time we are told that the people in some of the towns of Yorkshire cherished a prejudice so strong and violent against strangers and foreigners that one who ventured to pass through their streets would be pelted with stones.

Of all the races and varieties of men which have suffered from this feeling, the colored people of this country have endured most. They can resort to no disguises which will enable them to escape its deadly aim. They carry in front the evidence which marks them for persecution. They stand at the extreme point of difference from the Caucasian race, and their African origin can be instantly recognized, though they may be several removes from the typical African race. They may remonstrate like Shylock — "Hath not a Jew eyes? hath not a Jew hands, organs, dimensions, senses, affections, passions? fed with the same food, hurt with the same weapons, subject to the same diseases, healed by the same means, warmed and cooled by the same summer and winter, as a Christian is?" — but such eloquence is unavailing. They are negroes — and that is enough, in the eye of this unreasoning prejudice, to justify indignity and violence. In nearly every department of American life they are confronted by this insidious influence. It fills the air. It meets them at the workshop and factory, when they apply for work. It meets them at the church, at the hotel, at the ballot-box, and worst of all, it meets them in the jury-box. Without crime or offense against law or gospel, the colored man is the Jean Valjean of American society. He has escaped from the galleys, and hence all presumptions are against him. The workshop denies him work, and the inn denies him shelter; the ballot-box a fair vote, and the jury-box a fair trial. He has ceased to be the slave of society. He may not now be bought and sold like a beast in the market, but he is the trammeled victim of a prejudice, well calculated to repress his manly ambition, paralyze his energies, and make him a dejected and spiritless man, if not a sullen enemy to society, fit to prey upon life and property and to make trouble generally.

When this evil spirit is judge, jury, and prosecutor, nothing less than overwhelming evidence is sufficient to overcome the force of unfavorable presumptions.

Everything against the person with the hated color is promptly taken for granted; while everything in his favor is received with suspicion and doubt.

A boy of this color is found in his bed tied, mutilated, and bleeding, when forthwith all ordinary experience is set aside, and he is presumed to have been guilty of the outrage upon himself; weeks and months he is kept on trial for the offense, and every effort is made to entangle the poor fellow in the confused meshes of expert testimony (the least trustworthy of all evidence). This same spirit, which promptly assumes everything against us, just as readily denies or explains away everything in our favor. We are not, as a race, even permitted to appropriate the virtues and achievements of our individual representatives. Manliness, capacity, learning, laudable ambition, heroic service, by any of our number, are easily placed to the credit of the superior race. One drop of Teutonic blood is enough to account for all good and great qualities occasionally coupled with a colored skin; and on the other hand, one drop of negro blood, though in the veins of a man of Teutonic whiteness, is enough of which to predicate all offensive and ignoble qualities. In presence of this spirit, if a crime is committed, and the criminal is not positively known, a suspicious-looking colored man is sure to have been seen in the neighborhood. If an unarmed colored man is shot down and dies in his tracks, a jury, under the influence of this spirit, does not hesitate to find the murdered man the real criminal, and the murderer innocent.

Now let us examine this subject a little more closely. It is claimed that this wonder-working prejudice — this moral magic that can change virtue into vice, and innocence to crime; which makes the dead man the murderer, and holds the living homicide harmless — is a natural, instinctive, and invincible attribute of the white race, and one that cannot be eradicated; that even evolution itself cannot carry us beyond or above it. Alas for this poor suffering world (for four-fifths of mankind are colored), if this claim be true! In that case men are forever doomed to injustice, oppression, hate, and strife; and the religious sentiment of the world, with its grand idea of human brotherhood, its "peace on earth and good-will to men," and its golden rule, must be voted a dream, a delusion, and a snare.

But is this color prejudice the natural and inevitable thing it claims to be? If it is so, then it is utterly idle to write against it, preach, pray, or legislate against it, or pass constitutional amendments against it. Nature will have her course, and one might as well preach and pray to a horse against running, to a fish against swimming, or to a bird against flying. Fortunately, however, there is good ground for calling in question this high pretension of a vulgar and wicked prepossession.

If I could talk with all my white fellow-countrymen on this subject, I would say to them, in the language of Scripture: "Come and let us reason together." Now, without being too elementary and formal, it may be stated here that there are at least seven points which candid men will be likely to admit, but which, if admitted, will prove fatal to the popular thought and practice of the times.

First. If what we call prejudice against color be natural, i.e., a part of human nature itself, it follows that it must be co-extensive with human nature, and will and must manifest itself whenever and wherever the two races are brought into contact. It would not vary with either latitude, longitude, or altitude; but like fire and gunpowder, whenever brought together, there would be an explosion of contempt, aversion, and hatred.

Secondly. If it can be shown that there is anywhere on the globe any considerable country where the contact of the African and Caucasian is not distinguished by this explosion of race-wrath, there is reason to doubt that the prejudice is an ineradicable part of human nature.

Thirdly. If this so-called natural, instinctive prejudice can be satisfactorily accounted for by facts and considerations wholly apart from the color features of the respective races, thus placing it among the things subject to human volition and control, we may venture to deny the claim set up for it in the name of human nature.

Fourthly. If any considerable number of white people have overcome this prejudice in themselves, have cast it out as an unworthy sentiment, and have survived the operation, the fact shows that this prejudice is not at any rate a vital part of human nature, and may be eliminated from the race without harm.

Fifthly. If this prejudice shall, after all, prove to be, in its essence and in its natural manifestation, simply a prejudice against condition, and not against race or color, and that it disappears when this or that condition is absent, then the argument drawn from the nature of the Caucasian race falls to the ground.

Sixthly. If prejudice of race and color is only natural in the sense that ignorance, superstition, bigotry, and vice are natural, then it has no better defense than they, and should be despised and put away from human relations as an enemy to the peace, good order, and happiness of human society.

Seventhly. If, still further, this averson* to the negro arises out of the fact that he is as we see him, poor, spiritless, ignorant, and degraded, then whatever is humane, noble, and superior, in the mind of the superior and more fortunate race, will desire that all arbitrary barriers against his manhood, intelligence, and elevation shall be removed, and a fair chance in the race of life be given him.

The first of these propositions does not require discussion. It commends itself to the understanding at once. Natural qualities are common and universal, and do not change essentially on the mountain or in the valley. I come therefore to the second point — the existence of countries where this malignant prejudice, as we know it in America, does not prevail; where character, not color, is the passport to consideration; where the right of the black man to be a man, and a man among men, is not questioned; where he may, without offense, even presume to be a gentleman. That there are such countries in the world there is ample evidence. Intelligent and observing travelers, having no theory to support, men whose testimony would be received without question in respect of any other matter, and should not be questioned in this, tell us that they find no color prejudice in Europe, except among Americans who reside there. In England and on the Continent, the colored man is no more an object of hate than any other person. He mingles with the multitude unquestioned, without offense given or received. During the two years which the writer spent abroad, though he was much in society, and was sometimes in the company of lords and ladies, he does not remember one word, look, or gesture that indicated the slightest aversion to him on account of color. His experience was not in this respect exceptional or singular. Messrs. Remond, Ward, Garnet, Brown, Pennington, Crummell, and Bruce, all of them colored, and some of them black, bear the same testimony. If what these gentleman say (and it can be corroborated by a thousand witnesses) is true there is no prejudice against color in England, save as it is carried there by Americans — carried there as a moral disease from an infected country. It is American, not European; local, not general; limited, not universal, and must be ascribed to artificial conditions, and not to any fixed and universal law of nature.

The third point is: Can this prejudice against color, as it is called, be accounted for by circumstances outside and independent of race or color? If it can be thus explained, an incubus may be removed from the breasts of both the white and the black people of this country, as well as from that large intermediate population which has sprung up between these alleged irreconcilable extremes. It will help us to see that it is not necessary that the Ethiopian shall change his skin, nor needful that the white man shall change the essential elements of his nature, in order that mutual respect and consideration may exist between the two races.

Now it is easy to explain the conditions outside of race or color from which may spring feelings akin to those which we call prejudice. A man without the ability or the disposition to pay a just debt does not feel at ease in the presence of his creditor. He does not want to meet him on the street, or in the market-place. Such meeting makes him uncomfortable. He would rather find fault with the bill than pay the debt, and the creditor himself will soon develop in the eyes of the debtor qualities not altogether to his taste.

Some one has well said, we may easily forgive those who injure us, but it is hard to forgive those whom we injure. The greatest injury this side of death, which one human being can inflict on another, is to enslave him, to blot out his personality, degrade his manhood, and sink him to the condition of a beast of burden; and just this has been done here during more than two centuries. No other people under heaven, of whatever type or endowments, could have been so enslaved without falling into contempt and scorn on the part of those enslaving them. Their slavery would itself stamp them with odious features, and give their oppressors arguments in favor of oppression. Besides the long years of wrong and injury inflicted upon the colored race in this country, and the effect of these wrongs upon that race, morally, intellectually, and physically, corrupting their morals, darkening their minds, and twisting their bodies and limbs out of all approach to symmetry, there has been a mountain of gold — uncounted millions of dollars — resting upon them with crushing weight. During all the years of their bondage, the slave master had a direct interest in discrediting the personality of those he held as property. Every man who had a thousand dollars so invested had a thousand reasons for painting the black man as fit only for slavery. Having made him the companion of horses and mules, he naturally sought to justify himself by assuming that the negro was not much better than a mule. The holders of twenty hundred million dollars' worth of property in human chattels procured the means of influencing press, pulpit, and politician, and through these instrumentalities they belittled our virtues and magnified our vices, and have made us odious in the eyes of the world. Slavery had the power at one time to make and unmake Presidents, to construe the law, dictate the policy, set the fashion in national manners and customs, interpret the Bible, and control the church; and, naturally enough, the old masters set themselves up as much too high as they set the manhood of the negro too low. Out of the depths of slavery has come this prejudice and this color line. It is broad enough and black enough to explain all the malign influences which assail the newly emancipated millions to-day. In reply to this argument it will perhaps be said that the negro has no slavery now to contend with, and that having been free during the last sixteen years, he ought by this time to have contradicted the degrading qualities which slavery formerly ascribed to him. All very true as to the letter, but utterly false as to the spirit. Slavery is indeed gone, but its shadow still lingers over the country and poisons more or less the moral atmosphere of all sections of the republic. The money motive for assailing the negro which slavery represented is indeed absent, but love of power and dominion, strengthened by two centuries of irresponsible power, still remains.

Having now shown how slavery created and sustained this prejudice against race and color, and the powerful motive for its creation, the other four points made against it need not be discussed in detail and at length, but may only be referred to in a general way.

If what is called the instinctive aversion of the white race for the colored, when analyzed, is seen to be the same as that which men feel or have felt toward other objects wholly apart from color; if it should be the same as that sometimes exhibited by the haughty and rich to the humble and poor, the same as the Brahmin feels toward the lower caste, the same as the Norman felt toward the Saxon, the same as that cherished by the Turk against Christians, the same as Christians have felt toward the Jews, the same as that which murders a Christian in Wallachia, calls him a "dog" in Constantinople, oppresses and persecutes a Jew in Berlin, hunts down a socialist in St. Petersburg, drives a Hebrew from an hotel at Saratoga, that scorns the Irishman in London, the same as Catholics once felt for Protestants, the same as that which insults, abuses, and kills the Chinaman on the Pacific slope — then may we well enough affirm that this prejudice really has nothing whatever to do with race or color, and that it has its motive and mainspring in some other source with which the mere facts of color and race have nothing to do.

After all, some very well informed and very well meaning people will read what I have now said, and what seems to me so just and reasonable, and will still insist that the color of the negro has something to do with the feeling entertained toward him; that the white man naturally shudders at the thought of contact with one who is black — that the impulse is one which he can neither resist nor control. Let us see if this conclusion is a sound one. An argument is unsound when it proves too little or too much, or when it proves nothing. If color is an offense, it is so, entirely apart from the manhood it envelops. There must be something in color of itself to kindle rage and inflame hate, and render the white man generally uncomfortable. If the white man were really so constituted that color were, in itself, a torment to him, this grand old earth of ours would be no place for him. Colored objects confront him here at every point of the compass. If he should shrink and shudder every time he sees anything dark, he would have little time for anything else. He would require a colorless world to live in — a world where flowers, fields, and floods should all be of snowy whiteness; where rivers, lakes, and oceans should all be white; where all the men, and women, and children should be white; where all the fish of the sea, all the birds of the air, all the "cattle upon a thousand hills," should be white; where the heavens above and the earth beneath should be white, and where day and night should not be divided by light and darkness, but the world should be one eternal scene of light. In such a white world, the entrance of a black man would be hailed with joy by the inhabitants. Anybody or anything would be welcome that would break the oppressive and tormenting monotony of the all-prevailing white.

In the abstract, there is no prejudice against color. No man shrinks from another because he is clothed in a suit of black, nor offended with his boots because they are black. We are told by those who have resided there that a white man in Africa comes to think that ebony is about the proper color for man. Good old Thomas Whitson — a noble old Quaker — a man of rather odd appearance — used to say that even he would be handsome if he could change public opinion.

Aside from the curious contrast to himself, the white child feels nothing on the first sight of a colored man. Curiosity is the only feeling. The office of color in the color line is a very plain and subordinate one. It simply advertises the objects of oppression, insult, and persecution. It is not the maddening liquor, but the black letters on the sign telling the world where it may be had. It is not the hated Quaker, but the broad brim and the plain coat. It is not the hateful Cain, but the mark by which he is known. The color is innocent enough, but things with which it is coupled make it hated. Slavery, ignorance, stupidity, servility, poverty, dependence, are undesirable conditions. When these shall cease to be coupled with color, there will be no color line drawn. It may help in this direction to observe a few of the inconsistencies of the color-line feeling, for it is neither uniform in its operations nor consistent in its principles. Its contradictions in the latter respect would be amusing if the feeling itself were not so deserving of unqualified abhorrence. Our Californian brothers, of Hibernian descent, hate the Chinaman, and kill him, and when asked why they do so, their answer is that a Chinaman is so industrious he will do all the work, and can live by wages upon which other people would starve. When the same people and others are asked why they hate the colored people, the answer is that they are indolent and wasteful, and cannot take care of themselves. Statesmen of the South will tell you that the negro is too ignorant and stupid properly to exercise the elective franchise, and yet his greatest offense is that he acts with the only party intelligent enough in the eyes of the nation to legislate for the country. In one breath they tell us that the negro is so weak in intellect, and so destitute of manhood, that he is but the echo of designing white men, and yet in another they will virtually tell you that the negro is so clear in his moral perceptions, so firm in purpose, so steadfast in his convictions, that he cannot be persuaded by arguments or intimidated by threats, and that nothing but the shot-gun can restrain him from voting for the men and measures he approves. They shrink back in horror from contact with the negro as a man and a gentleman, but like him very well as a barber, waiter, coachman, or cook. As a slave, he could ride anywhere, side by side with his white master, but as a freeman, he must be thrust into the smoking-car. As a slave, he could go into the first cabin; as a freeman, he was not allowed abaft the wheel. Formerly it was said he was incapable of learning, and at the same time it was a crime against the State for any man to teach him to read. To-day he is said to be originally and permanently inferior to the white race, and yet wild apprehensions are expressed lest six millions of this inferior race will somehow or other manage to rule over thirty-five millions of the superior race. If inconsistency can prove the hollowness of anything, certainly the emptiness of this pretense that color has any terrors is easily shown. The trouble is that most men, and especially mean men, want to have something under them. The rich man would have the poor man, the white would have the black, the Irish would have the negro, and the negro must have a dog, if he can get nothing higher in the scale of intelligence to dominate. This feeling is one of the vanities which enlightenment will dispel. A good but simple-minded Abolitionist said to me that he was not ashamed to walk with me down Broadway arm-in-arm, in open daylight, and evidently thought he was saying something that must be very pleasing to my self-importance, but it occurred to me, at the moment, this man does not dream of any reason why I might be ashamed to walk arm-in-arm with him through Broadway in open daylight. Riding in a stage-coach from Concord, New Hampshire, to Vergennes, Vermont, many years ago, I found myself on very pleasant terms with all the passengers through the night, but the morning light came to me as it comes to the stars; I was as Dr. Beecher says he was at the first fire he witnessed, when a bucket of cold water was poured down his back — "the fire was not put out, but he was." The fact is, the higher the colored man rises in the scale of society, the less prejudice does he meet.

The writer has met and mingled freely with the leading great men of his time, — at home and abroad, in public halls and private houses, on the platform and at the fireside, — and can remember no instance when among such men has he been made to feel himself an object of aversion. Men who are really great are too great to be small. This was gloriously true of the late Abraham Lincoln, William H. Seward, Salmon P. Chase, Henry Wilson, John P. Hale, Lewis Tappan, Edmund Quincy, Joshua R. Giddings, Gerrit Smith, and Charles Sumner, and many others among the dead. Good taste will not permit me now to speak of the living, except to say that the number of those who rise superior to prejudice is great and increasing. Let those who wish to see what is to be the future of America, as relates to races and race relations, attend, as I have attended, during the administration of President Hayes, the grand diplomatic receptions at the executive mansion, and see there, as I have seen, in its splendid east room, the wealth, culture, refinement, and beauty of the nation assembled, and with it the eminent representatives of other nations, — the swarthy Turk with his "fez," the Englishman shining with gold, the German, the Frenchman, the Spaniard, the Japanese, the Chinaman, the Caucasian, the Mongolian, the Sandwich Islander, and the negro, — all moving about freely, each respecting the rights and dignity of the other, and neither receiving nor giving offense.

"Then let us pray that come it may,
As come it will for a' that,
That sense and worth, o'er a' the earth,
May bear the gree, and a' that;
"That man to man, the world o'er,
Shall brothers be, for a' that."

The Future of the Colored Race

(1886)

It is quite impossible, at this early date, to say with any decided emphasis what the future of the colored people will be. Speculations of that kind, thus far, have only reflected the mental bias and education of the many who have essayed to solve the problem.

We all know what the negro has been as a slave. In this relation we have his experience of two hundred and fifty years before us, and can easily know the character and qualities he has developed and exhibited during this long and severe ordeal. In his new relation to his environments, we see him only in the twilight of twenty years of semi-freedom; for he has scarcely been free long enough to outgrow the marks of the lash on his back and the fetters on his limbs. He stands before us, to-day, physically, a maimed and mutilated man. His mother was lashed to agony before the birth of her babe, and the bitter anguish of the mother is seen in the countenance of her offspring. Slavery has twisted his limbs, shattered his feet, deformed his body and distorted his features. He remains black, but no longer comely. Sleeping on the dirt floor of the slave cabin in infancy, cold on one side and warm on the other, a forced circulation of blood on the one side and chilled and retarded circulation on the other, it has come to pass that he has not the vertical bearing of a perfect man. His lack of symmetry, caused by no fault of his own, creates a resistance to his progress which cannot well be overestimated, and should be taken into account, when measuring his speed in the new race of life upon which he has now entered. As I have often said before, we should not measure the negro from the heights which the white race has attained, but from the depths from which he has come. You will not find Burke, Grattan, Curran and O'Connell among the oppressed and famished poor of the famine-stricken districts of Ireland. Such men come of comfortable antecedents and sound parents.

Laying aside all prejudice in favor of or against race, looking at the negro as politically and socially related to the American people generally, and measuring the forces arrayed against him, I do not see how he can survive and flourish in this country as a distinct and separate race, nor do I see how he can be removed from the country either by annihilation or expatriation.

Sometimes I have feared that, in some wild paroxysm of rage, the white race, forgetful of the claims of humanity and the precepts of the Christian religion, will proceed to slaughter the negro in wholesale, as some of that race have attempted to slaughter Chinamen, and as it has been done in detail in some districts of the Southern States. The grounds of this fear, however, have in some measure decreased, since the negro has largely disappeared from the arena of Southern politics, and has betaken himself to industrial pursuits and the acquisition of wealth and education, though even here, if over-prosperous, he is likely to excite a dangerous antagonism; for the white people do not easily tolerate the presence among them of a race more prosperous than themselves. The negro as a poor ignorant creature does not contradict the race pride of the white race. He is more a source of amusement to that race than an object of resentment. Malignant resistance is augmented as he approaches the plane occupied by the white race, and yet I think that that resistance will gradually yield to the pressure of wealth, education, and high character.

My strongest conviction as to the future of the negro therefore is, that he will not be expatriated nor annihilated, nor will he forever remain a separate and distinct race from the people around him, but that he will be absorbed, assimilated, and will only appear finally, as the Phoenicians now appear on the shores of the Shannon, in the features of a blended race. I cannot give at length my reasons for this conclusion, and perhaps the reader may think that the wish is father to the thought, and may in his wrath denounce my conclusion as utterly impossible. To such I would say, tarry a little, and look at the facts. Two hundred years ago there were two distinct and separate streams of human life running through this country. They stood at opposite extremes of ethnological classification: all black on the one side, all white on the other. Now, between these two extremes, an intermediate race has arisen, which is neither white nor black, neither Caucasian nor Ethiopian, and this intermediate race is constantly increasing. I know it is said that marital alliance between these races is unnatural, abhorrent and impossible; but exclamations of this kind only shake the air. They prove nothing against a stubborn fact like that which confronts us daily and which is open to the observation of all. If this blending of the two races were impossible we should not have at least one-fourth of our colored population composed of persons of mixed blood, ranging all the way from a dark-brown color to the point where there is no visible admixture. Besides, it is obvious to common sense that there is no need of the passage of laws, or the adoption of other devices, to prevent what is in itself impossible.

Of course this result will not be reached by any hurried or forced processes. It will not arise out of any theory of the wisdom of such blending of the two races. If it comes at all, it will come without shock or noise or violence of any kind, and only in the fullness of time, and it will be so adjusted to surrounding conditions as hardly to be observed. I would not be understood as advocating intermarriage between the two races. I am not a propagandist, but a prophet. I do not say that what I say should come to pass, but what I think is likely to come to pass, and what is inevitable. While I would not be understood as advocating the desirability of such a result, I would not be understood as deprecating it. Races and varieties of the human family appear and disappear, but humanity remains and will remain forever. The American people will one day be truer to this idea than now, and will say with Scotia's inspired son:

"A man's a man for a' that."

When that day shall come, they will not pervert and sin against the verity of language as they now do by calling a man of mixed blood, a negro; they will tell the truth. It is only prejudice against the negro which calls every one, however nearly connected with the white race, and however remotely connected with the negro race, a negro. The motive is not a desire to elevate the negro, but to humiliate and degrade those of mixed blood; not a desire to bring the negro up, but to cast the mulatto and the quadroon down by forcing him below an arbitrary and hated color line. Men of mixed blood in this country apply the name "negro" to themselves, not because it is a correct ethnological description, but to seem especially devoted to the black side of their parentage. Hence in some cases they are more noisily opposed to the conclusion to which I have come, than either the white or the honestly black race. The opposition to amalgamation, of which we hear so much on the part of colored people, is for most part the merest affectation, and, will never form an impassable barrier to the union of the two varieties.

A Plea for Free Speech

(1860)

Boston is a great city — and Music Hall has a fame almost as extensive as that of Boston. Nowhere more than here have the principles of human freedom been expounded. But for the circumstances already mentioned, it would seem almost presumption for me to say anything here about those principles. And yet, even here, in Boston, the moral atmosphere is dark and heavy. The principles of human liberty, even I correctly apprehended, find but limited support in this hour a trial. The world moves slowly, and Boston is much like the world. We thought the principle of free speech was an accomplished fact. Here, if nowhere else, we thought the right of the people to assemble and to express their opinion was secure. Dr. Channing had defended the right, Mr. Garrison had practically asserted the right, and Theodore Parker had maintained it with steadiness and fidelity to the last.

But here we are to-day contending for what we thought we gained years ago. The mortifying and disgraceful fact stares us in the face, that though Faneuil Hall and Bunker Hill Monument stand, freedom of speech is struck down. No lengthy detail of facts is needed. They are already notorious; far more so than will be wished ten years hence.

The world knows that last Monday a meeting assembled to discuss the question: "How Shall Slavery Be Abolished?" The world also knows that that meeting was invaded, insulted, captured by a mob of gentlemen, and thereafter broken up and dispersed by the order of the mayor, who refused to protect it, though called upon to do so. If this had been a mere outbreak of passion and prejudice among the baser sort, maddened by rum and hounded on by some wily politician to serve some immediate purpose, — a mere exceptional affair, — it might be allowed to rest with what has already been said. But the leaders of the mob were gentlemen. They were men who pride themselves upon their respect for law and order.

These gentlemen brought their respect for the law with them and proclaimed it loudly while in the very act of breaking the law. Theirs was the law of slavery. The law of free speech and the law for the protection of public meetings they trampled under foot, while they greatly magnified the law of slavery.

The scene was an instructive one. Men seldom see such a blending of the gentleman with the rowdy, as was shown on that occasion. It proved that human nature is very much the same, whether in tarpaulin or broadcloth. Nevertheless, when gentlemen approach us in the character of lawless and abandoned loafers, — assuming for the moment their manners and tempers, — they have themselves to blame if they are estimated below their quality.

No right was deemed by the fathers of the Government more sacred than the right of speech. It was in their eyes, as in the eyes of all thoughtful men, the great moral renovator of society and government. Daniel Webster called it a homebred right, a fireside privilege. Liberty is meaningless where the right to utter one's thoughts and opinions has ceased to exist. That, of all rights, is the dread of tyrants. It is the right which they first of all strike down. They know its power. Thrones, dominions, principalities, and powers, founded in injustice and wrong, are sure to tremble, if men are allowed to reason of righteousness, temperance, and of a judgment to come in their presence. Slavery cannot tolerate free speech. Five years of its exercise would banish the auction block and break every chain in the South. They will have none of it there, for they have the power. But shall it be so here?

Even here in Boston, and among the friends of freedom, we hear two voices: one denouncing the mob that broke up our meeting on Monday as a base and cowardly outrage; and another, deprecating and regretting the holding of such a meeting, by such men, at such a time. We are told that the meeting was ill-timed, and the parties to it unwise.

Why, what is the matter with us? Are we going to palliate and excuse a palpable and flagrant outrage on the right of speech, by implying that only a particular description of persons should exercise that right? Are we, at such a time, when a great principle has been struck down, to quench the moral indignation which the deed excites, by casting reflections upon those on whose persons the outrage has been committed? After all the arguments for liberty to which Boston has listened for more than a quarter of a century, has she yet to learn that the time to assert a right is the time when the right itself is called in question, and that the men of all others to assert it are the men to whom the right has been denied?

It would be no vindication of the right of speech to prove that certain gentlemen of great distinction, eminent for their learning and ability, are allowed to freely express their opinions on all subjects — including the subject of slavery. Such a vindication would need, itself, to be vindicated. It would add insult to injury. Not even an old-fashioned abolition meeting could vindicate that right in Boston just now. There can be no right of speech where any man, however lifted up, or however humble, however young, or however old, is overawed by force, and compelled to suppress his honest sentiments.

Equally clear is the right to hear. To suppress free speech is a double wrong. It violates the rights of the hearer as well as those of the speaker. It is just as criminal to rob a man of his right to speak and hear as it would be to rob him of his money. I have no doubt that Boston will vindicate this right. But in order to do so, there must be no concessions to the enemy. When a man is allowed to speak because he is rich and powerful, it aggravates the crime of denying the right to the poor and humble.

The principle must rest upon its own proper basis. And until the right is accorded to the humblest as freely as to the most exalted citizen, the government of Boston is but an empty name, and its freedom a mockery. A man's right to speak does not depend upon where he was born or upon his color. The simple quality of manhood is the solid basis of the right — and there let it rest forever.

The Church and Prejudice

(Speech delivered at the Plymouth County Anti-Slavery Society,
November 4, 1841)

At the South I was a member of the Methodist Church. When I
came north, I thought one Sunday I would attend communion, at one of
the churches of my denomination, in the town I was staying. The white
people gathered round the altar, the blacks clustered by the door. After
the good minister had served out the bread and wine to one portion of
those near him, he said, "These may withdraw, and others come forward;"
thus he proceeded till all the white members had been served. Then he
took a long breath, and looking out towards the door, exclaimed, "Come
up, colored friends, come up! for you know God is no respecter of persons!"
I haven't been there to see the sacraments taken since.

At New Bedford, where I live, there was a great revival of religion
not long ago—many were converted and "received" as they said, "into the
kingdom of heaven." But it seems, the kingdom of heaven is like a net; at
least so it was according to the practice of these pious Christians; and
when the net was drawn ashore, they had to set down and cull out the
fish. Well, it happened now that some of the fish had rather black scales;
so these were sorted out and packed by themselves. But among those who
experienced religion at this time was a colored girl; she was baptized in
the same water as the rest; so she thought she might sit at the Lord's
table and partake of the same sacramental elements with the others. The
deacon handed round the cup, and when he came to the black girl, he
could not pass her, for there was the minister looking right at him, and as
he was a kind of abolitionist, the deacon was rather afraid of giving him
offense; so he handed the girl the cup, and she tasted. Now it so happened
that next to her sat a young lady who had been converted at the same
time, baptized in the same water, and put her trust in the same blessed
Saviour; yet when the cup containing the precious blood which had been
shed for all, came to her, she rose in disdain, and walked out of the
church. Such was the religion she had experienced!

Another young lady fell into a trance. When she awoke, she declared
she had been to heaven. Her friends were all anxious to know what and
whom she had seen there; so she told the whole story. But there was one
good old lady whose curiosity went beyond that of all the others—and she
inquired of the girl that had the vision, if she saw any black folks in
heaven? After some hesitation, the reply was, "Oh! I didn't go into the
kitchen!"

Thus you see, my hearers, this prejudice goes even into the church
of God. And there are those who carry it so far that it is disagreeable to
them even to think of going to heaven, if colored people are going there
too. And whence comes it? The grand cause is slavery; but there are

others less prominent; one of them is the way in which children in this part of the country are instructed to regard the blacks.

"Yes!" exclaimed an old gentleman, interrupting him—"when they behave wrong, they are told, 'black man come catch you.'"

Yet people in general will say they like colored men as well as any other, but in their proper place! They assign us that place; they don't let us do it for ourselves, nor will they allow us a voice in the decision. They will not allow that we have a head to think, and a heart to feel, and a soul to aspire. They treat us not as men, but as dogs—they cry "Stu-boy!" and expect us to run and do their bidding. That's the way we are liked. You degrade us, and then ask why we are degraded—you shut our mouths, and then ask why we don't speak—you close our colleges and seminaries against us, and then ask why we don't know more.

But all this prejudice sinks into insignificance in my mind, when compared with the enormous iniquity of the system which is its cause—the system that sold my four sisters and my brothers into bondage—and which calls in its priests to defend it even from the Bible! The slaveholding ministers preach up the divine right of the slaveholders to property in their fellow- men. The southern preachers say to the poor slave, "Oh! if you wish to be happy in time, happy in eternity, you must be obedient to your masters; their interest is yours. God made one portion of men to do the working, and another to do the thinking; how good God is! Now, you have no trouble or anxiety; but ah! you can't imagine how perplexing it is to your masters and mistresses to have so much thinking to do in your behalf! You cannot appreciate your blessings; you know not how happy a thing it is for you, that you were born of that portion of the human family which has the working, instead of the thinking to do! Oh! how grateful and obedient you ought to be to your masters! How beautiful are the arrangements of Providence! Look at your hard, horny hands—see how nicely they are adapted to the labor you have to perform! Look at our delicate fingers, so exactly fitted for our station, and see how manifest it is that God designed us to be His thinkers, and you the workers—Oh! the wisdom of God!"—I used to attend a Methodist church, in which my master was a class leader; he would talk most sanctimoniously about the dear Redeemer, who was sent "to preach deliverance to the captives, and set at liberty them that are bruised"—he could pray at morning, pray at noon, and pray at night; yet he could lash up my poor cousin by his two thumbs, and inflict stripes and blows upon his bare back, till the blood streamed to the ground! all the time quoting scripture, for his authority, and appealing to that passage of the Holy Bible which says, "He that knoweth his master's will, and doeth it not, shall be beaten with many stripes!" Such was the amount of this good Methodist's piety.

Fighting Rebels with Only One Hand

(Douglass' Monthly, September 1861)

What on earth is the matter with the American Government and people? Do they really covet the world's ridicule as well as their own social and political ruin? What are they thinking about, or don't they condescend to think at all? So, indeed, it would seem from their blindness in dealing with the tremendous issue now upon them. Was there ever anything like it before? They are sorely pressed on every hand by a vast army of slaveholding rebels, flushed with success, and infuriated by the darkest inspirations of a deadly hate, bound to rule or ruin. Washington, the seat of Government, after ten thousand assurances to the contrary, is now positively in danger of falling before the rebel army. Maryland, a little while ago considered safe for the Union, is now admitted to be studded with the materials for insurrection, and which may flame forth at any moment.—Every resource of the nation, whether of men or money, whether of wisdom or strength, could be well employed to avert the impending ruin. Yet most evidently the demands of the hour are not comprehended by the Cabinet or the crowd. Our Presidents, Governors, Generals and Secretaries are calling, with almost frantic vehemance, for men.—"Men! men! send us men!" they scream, or the cause of the Union is gone, the life of a great nation is ruthlessly sacrificed, and the hopes of a great nation go out in darkness; and yet these very officers, representing the people and Government, steadily and persistently refuse to receive the very class of men which have a deeper interest in the defeat and humiliation of the rebels, than all others.—Men are wanted in Missouri—wanted in Western Virginia, to hold and defend what has been already gained; they are wanted in Texas, and all along the sea coast, and though the Government has at its command a class in the country deeply interested in suppressing the insurrection, it sternly refuses to summon from among the vast multitude a single man, and degrades and insults the whole class by refusing to allow any of their number to defend with their strong arms and brave hearts the national cause. What a spectacle of blind, unreasoning prejudice and pusillanimity is this! The national edifice is on fire. Every man who can carry a bucket of water, or remove a brick, is wanted; but those who have the care of the building, having a profound respect for the feeling of the national burglars who set the building on fire, are determined that the flames shall only be extinguished by Indo-Caucasian hands, and to have the building burnt rather than save it by means of any other. Such is the pride, the stupid prejudice and folly that rules the hour.

Why does the Government reject the Negro? Is he not a man? Can he not wield a sword, fire a gun, march and countermarch, and obey orders like any other? Is there the least reason to believe that a regiment of well-drilled Negroes would deport themselves less soldier-like on the battlefield than the raw troops gathered up generally from the towns and cities of the State of New York? We do believe that such soldiers, if allowed to take up arms in defence of the Government, and made to feel that they are hereafter to be recognized as persons having rights, would set the highest example of order and general good behavior to their fellow soldiers, and in every way add to the national power.

If persons so humble as we can be allowed to speak to the President of the United States, we should ask him if this dark and terrible hour of the nation's extremity is a time for consulting a mere vulgar and unnatural prejudice? We should ask him if national preservation and necessity were not better guides in this emergency than either the tastes of the rebels, or the pride and prejudices of the vulgar? We would tell him that General Jackson in a slave state fought side by side with Negroes at New Orleans, and like a true man, despising meanness, he bore testimony to their bravery at the close of the war. We would tell him that colored men in Rhode Island and Connecticut performed their full share in the war of the Revolution, and that men of the same color, such as the noble Shields Green, Nathaniel Turner and Denmark Vesey stand ready to peril everything at the command of the Government. We would tell him that this is no time to fight with one hand, when both are needed; that this is no time to fight only with your white hand, and allow your black hand to remain tied.

Whatever may be the folly and absurdity of the North, the South at least is true and wise. The Southern papers no longer indulge in the vulgar expression, "free n——rs." That class of bipeds are now called "colored residents." The Charleston papers say:

"The colored residents of this city can challenge comparison with their class, in any city or town, in loyalty or devotion to the cause of the South. Many of them individually, and without ostentation, have been contributing liberally, and on Wednesday evening, the 7th inst., a very large meeting was held by them, and a committee appointed to provide for more efficient aid. The proceedings of the meeting will appear in results hereinafter to be reported."

It is now pretty well established, that there are at the present moment many colored men in the Confederate army doing duty not only as cooks, servants and laborers, but as real soldiers, having muskets on their shoulders, and bullets in their pockets, ready to shoot down loyal troops, and do all that soldiers may to destroy the Federal Government and build up that of the traitors and rebels. There were such soldiers at Manassas, and they are probably there still. There is a Negro in the army as well as in the fence, and our Government is likely to find it out before the war comes to an end. That the Negroes are numerous in the rebel army, and do for that army its heaviest work, is beyond question. They have been the chief laborers upon those temporary defences in which the rebels have been able to mow down our men. Negroes helped to build the batteries at Charleston. They relieve their gentlemanly and military masters from the stiffening drudgery of the camp, and devote them to the nimble and dexterous use of arms. Rising above vulgar prejudice, the slaveholding rebel accepts the aid of the black man as readily as that of any other. If a bad cause can do this, why should a good cause be less wisely conducted? We insist upon it, that one black regiment in such a war as this is, without being any more brave and orderly, would be worth to the Government more than two of any other; and that, while the Government continues to refuse the aid of colored men, thus alienating them from the national cause, and giving the rebels the advantage of them, it will not deserve better fortunes than it has thus far experienced.—Men in earnest don't fight with one hand, when they might fight with two, and a man drowning would not refuse to be saved even by a colored hand.

The Negro Exodus from the Gulf States

The negro, long deemed too indolent and stupid to discover and adopt any rational measure to secure and defend his rights as a man, may now be congratulated upon the telling contradiction which he has recently and strikingly given to this withering disparagement and reproach. He has discovered and adopted a measure which may assist very materially in the solution of some of the vital problems involved in his sudden elevation from slavery to freedom. He has shown that Mississippi can originate more than one plan, and that there is a possible plan for the oppressed as well as for the oppressor. He has not chosen to copy the example of his would-be enslavers. It is to his credit that he has steadily refused to resort to those extreme measures of repression and retaliation to which the cruel wrongs he has suffered might have tempted a less docile and forgiving race. He has not imitated the plan of the oppressed tenant, who sneaks in ambush and shoots his landlord, as in Ireland; nor the example of the Indian, who meets the invader of his hunting-ground with scalping-knife and tomahawk; he has not learned his lesson from the freed serfs of Russia, and organized assassination against tyrant princes and nobles; nor has he copied the example of his own race in Santa Domingo, who taught their French oppressors by fire and sword the danger of goading too far "the energy that slumbers in the black man's arm." On the contrary, he has adopted a simple, lawful and peaceable measure. It is emigration — the quiet withdrawal of his valuable bones and muscles from a condition of things which he considers no longer tolerable. Innocent as this remedy is for the manifold ills which he has thus far borne with marvelous patience, it is none the less significant and effective.

Nothing has occurred since the abolition of slavery which has excited a deeper interest among thoughtful men in all sections of the country than has this "exodus." In the simple fact that a few thousand freedmen have deliberately laid down the shovel and the hoe, quitted the sugar and cotton-fields of Mississippi and Louisiana, and sought homes in Kansas, and that thousands more are seriously meditating upon following their example, the sober thinking minds of the South have discovered a new and startling peril to the welfare of that section of our country. Already apprehension and alarm have led to noisy and frantic efforts on the part of the South to arrest and put an end to what it considers a depleting and ruinous evil.

It cannot be denied that there is much reason for this apprehension and alarm. This exodus has revealed to Southern men the humiliating fact that the prosperity and civilization of the South are at the mercy of the despised and hated negro — that it is for him more than for any other to say what shall be the future of the late Confederate States; that within their ample borders he alone can stand between the contending powers of savage and civilized life; that the giving or withholding of his labor will bless or blast their beautiful country.

Important as manual labor is everywhere, it is nowhere more important and absolutely indispensable to the existence of society than in the more southern of the United States. Machinery may continue to do — as it has done — much of the work of the North; but the work of the South requires bone, sinew and muscle of the strongest and most enduring kind for its performance. Labor in that section must know no pause. Her soil is pregnant and prolific with life and energy. All the forces of nature within her borders are wonderfully vigorous, persistent and active. Aided by an almost perpetual Summer, abundantly supplied with heat and moisture, her soil readily and rapidly covers itself with noxious weeds, dense forests and impenetrable jungles. Only a few years of non-tillage would be required to give the sunny and fruitful South to the bats and owls of a desolate wilderness. From this condition, shocking for a Southern man to contemplate, it is now seen that nothing less powerful than the naked iron arm of the negro can save her. For him, as a Southern laborer, there is no competitor or substitute. The thought of filling his place by any other variety of the human family, will be found delusive and utterly impracticable. Neither Chinaman, German, Norwegian nor Swede can drive him from the sugar and cotton-fields of Louisiana and Mississippi. They would certainly perish in the black bottoms of these States if they could be induced, which they cannot, to try the experiment.

Nature itself, in those States, comes to the rescue of the negro, fights his battles and enables him to exact conditions from those who would unfairly treat and oppress him. Besides being dependent upon the roughest and flintiest kind of labor, the climate of the South makes such labor uninviting and harshly repulsive to the white man. He dreads it, shrinks from it, and refuses it. He shuns the burning sun of the fields, and seeks the shade of the verandas. On the contrary, the negro walks, labors and sleeps in the sunlight unharmed. The standing apology for slavery was based upon a knowledge of this fact. It was said that the world must have cotton and sugar, and that only the negro could supply this want; and that he could be induced to do it only under the "beneficent whip" of some bloodthirsty Legree. The last part of this argument has been happily disproved by the large crops of these productions since Emancipation; but the first part of it stands firm, unassailed and unassailable.

Even if climatic and other natural causes did not protect the negro from all competition in the labor-market of the South, inevitable social causes would probably effect the same result. The slave system of that section has left behind it — as in the nature of the case it must — manners, customs and conditions to which free white laboring men will be in no haste to submit themselves and their families. They do not emigrate from the free North, where labor is respected, to a lately enslaved South, where labor has been whipped, chained and degraded for centuries. Naturally enough, such emigration follows the lines of latitude in which they who compose it were born. Not from South to North, but from East to West, "the Star of Empire takes its way."

Hence it is seen that the dependence of the planters, landowners and old master-class of the South upon the negro, however galling and humiliating to Southern pride and power, is nearly complete and perfect. There is only one mode of escape for them, and that mode they will certainly not adopt. It is to take off their own coats, cease to whittle sticks and talk politics at the cross-roads, and go themselves to work in their broad and sunny fields of cotton and sugar. An invitation to do this is about as harsh and distasteful to all their inclinations as would be an invitation to step down into their graves. With the negro, all this is different. Neither natural, artificial nor traditional causes stand in the way of the freedman to such labor in the South. Neither the heat nor the fever-demon which lurks in her tangled and cozy swamps affright him, and he stands to-day the admitted author of whatever of prosperity, beauty and civilization are now

possessed by the South, and the admitted arbiter of her destiny.

This, then, is the high vantage-ground of the negro: he has labor, the South wants it, and must have it or perish. Since he is free he can now give it or withhold it, use it where he is, or take it elsewhere, as he pleases. His labor made him a slave, and his labor can, if he will, make him free, comfortable and independent. It is more to him than fire, swords, ballot-boxes or bayonets. It touches the heart of the South through its pocket. This power served him well years ago, when in the bitterest extremity of his destitution. But for it he would have perished when he dropped out of slavery. It saved him then, and it will save him again. Emancipation came to him, surrounded by exceedingly unfriendly circumstances. It was not the choice or consent of the people among whom he lived, but against their will and a death-struggle on their part to prevent it. His chains were broken in the tempest and whirlwind of civil war. Without food, without shelter, without land, without money, and without friends, he, with his children, his sick, his aged and helpless ones, were turned loose and naked to the open sky. The announcement of his freedom was instantly followed by an order from his master to quit his old quarters and to seek bread thereafter from the hands of those who had given him his freedom. A desperate extremity was thus forced upon him at the outset of his freedom, and the world watched, with humane anxiety, to see what would become of him. His peril was imminent. Starvation and death stared him in the face, and marked him for their victim.

It will not be soon forgotten that, at the close of a five-hours' speech by the late Senator Sumner, in which he advocated with unequaled learning and eloquence the enfranchisement of the freedmen, the best argument with which he was met, in the Senate, was that legislation at that point would be utterly superfluous; that the negro was rapidly dying out, and must inevitably and speedily disappear and become extinct.

Inhuman and shocking as was this consignment of millions of human beings to extinction, the extremity of the negro, at that date, did not contradict, but favored, the prophecy. The policy of the old master class, dictated by passion, pride and revenge, was then to make the freedom of the negro a greater calamity to him, if possible, than had been his slavery. But, happily, both for the old master class and for the recently emancipated, there came then, as there will come now, the sober second thought. The old master class then found that it had made a great mistake. It had driven away the means of its own support. It had destroyed the hands and left the mouths. It had starved the negro, and starved itself. Not even to gratify its own anger and resentment could it afford to allow its fields to go uncultivated, and its tables to go unsupplied with food. Hence the freedman, less from humanity than cupidity, less from choice than necessity, was speedily called back to labor and life.

But now, after fourteen years of service, and fourteen years of separation from the visible presence of slavery, during which he has shown both disposition and ability to supply the labor-market of the South, and that he could do so far better as a freedman than he ever did as a slave; that more cotton and sugar can be raised by the same hands, under the inspiration of liberty and hope, than can be raised under the influence of bondage and the whip, he is again, alas! in the deepest trouble — again without a home, out under the open sky, with his wife and his little ones. He lines the sunny banks of the Mississippi, fluttering in rags and wretchedness, mournfully imploring hard-hearted steamboat captains to take him on board; while the friends of the emigration movement are diligently soliciting funds all over the North to help him away from his old home to the new Canaan of Kansas.

Several causes have been assigned for this truly desperate and pitiable spectacle. Many of these are, upon their faces, superficial, insufficient and ridiculous. Adepts in political trickery and duplicity, who will never go straight to a point when they can go crooked, explain the exodus as a cunning scheme to force a certain nomination upon the Republican party in 1890. It does not appear how such an effect is to follow such a cause. For if the negroes are to leave the South, as the advocates of exodus tell us, and settle in the North, where all their rights are protected — if this is the remedy for all the ills of the negro, the country need not trouble itself about securing a President whose chief recommendation is supposed to be his will and power to protect the negro in the South, and the nomination is thus rendered unnecessary by the success of the measure which made it necessary.

Again, we are told that greedy speculators in Kansas have adopted this plan to sell and increase the value of their lands. This cannot be true. Men of that class are usually shrewd. They do not seek to sell land to those who have no money, and they are too sharp to believe that they can increase the value of their property by inviting to its neighborhood a class of people against whom there is an intense and bitter popular prejudice. So far from speculating in the negro, and attempting to increase their wealth by promoting this stampede, the negro has been a heavy charge upon Kansas. Her benevolence and welcome to these homeless emigrants has been large, beautiful and touching.

Malignant emissaries from the North, it is said, have been circulating among the freedmen, talking to them and deluding them with promises of the great things which will be done for them if they will only go to Kansas. Plainly enough this theory fails for the want of even the show of probable motive. The North can have no motive to cripple industry at the South, or elsewhere in this country. If she were malignant enough, which she is not, she is not blind enough to her own interests to do any such thing. She sees and feels that an injury to any part of this country is an injury to the whole of it.

Again, it is said that this exodus is all the work of the defeated and disappointed demagogues, white and black, who have been hurled from place and power by the men of property and intelligence in the South. There may be some truth in this theory. Human nature is capable of resentment. It would not be strange if people who have been degraded and driven from place and power by brute force and by fraud, were to resent the outrage in this and in any way open to them.

But it is still further said that the exodus is peculiarly the work of Senator Windom. His resolution and speech in the Senate last Winter, it is said, has set this black ball in motion, and much wrath has been poured out upon that able and humane gentleman for his part in the movement. It need not be denied that there is truth in this allegation. Senator Windom's speech and resolution certainly did serve as a powerful stimulus to this emigration. Until he spoke, there was no general stampede from the cotton and sugar plantations of Mississippi and Louisiana. There can be no doubt, either, that the freedmen received erroneous notions, from some quarter, of what the Government was likely to do for them in the new country to which they were now going. They may have been told the story of "forty acres and a mule," and some of them may have believed and acted upon that story. But it is manifest that the real cause of this extraordinary exodus lies deeper down than any point touched by any of the causes thus far alleged. Political tricksters, land speculators, defeated office-seekers, Northern malignants, speeches and resolutions in the Senate or elsewhere, unaided by other causes, could not have, of themselves, set such a multitudinous exodus in motion.

The colored race is a remarkably home-loving race. It has done little in the way of voluntary colonization. It shrinks from the untried and unknown. It thinks its own locality the best in the world. Of all the galling conditions to which the negro was subjected in the days of his bondage, the one most galling to him was the liability of separation from home and friends. His love of home and his dread of change made him even partially content in slavery. He could endure the smart of the lash, could work to the utmost of his power, and be content, till the thought of being sent away from the scenes of his childhood and youth was thrust upon his heart. This was ever too much for him.

But argument is less needed upon this point than testimony. We have the story of the emigrants themselves, and if any can reveal the true cause of this exodus, they can. They have spoken, and their story is before the country. It is a sad story, disgraceful and scandalous to our age and country. Much of their testimony has been given under the solemnity of an oath.

They tell us, with great unanimity, that they are very badly treated at the South. The landowners, planters, and the old master class generally, deal unfairly with them; that having had their labor for nothing when they were slaves, these men now endeavor, by various devices, to get it for next to nothing; that, work as hard, faithfully and constantly as they may, live as plainly and as sparingly as they may, they are no better off at the end of the year than at the beginning; that they are the dupes and victims of cunning and fraud, in signing contracts which they cannot read and cannot fully understand; that they are compelled to trade at stores owned in whole or in part by their employers, and that they are paid with orders, and not with money.

They say they have to pay double the value of nearly everything they buy; that they are compelled to pay a rental of ten dollars a year for an acre of ground that will not bring thirty dollars under the hammer; that land-owners are in league to prevent land-owning by negroes; that when they work the land on shares, they barely make a living; that outside the towns and cities no provision is made for their education; and, ground down as they are, they cannot themselves employ teachers to teach their children; that they are not only the victims of fraud and cunning, but of violence and intimidation; that from their very poverty the temples of justice are not open to them; that the jury-box is virtually closed to them; that the murder of a black man by a white man is followed by no conviction or punishment. That for a crime for which a white man goes free, a black man is severely punished; that impunity and encouragement are given by the wealthy and respectable classes to men of the "baser sort," who delight in midnight raids upon the defenseless; that their ignorance of letters has put them at the mercy of men bent upon making their freedom a greater evil to them than was their slavery; that the law is the refuge of crime rather than of innocence; that even the old slave-driver's whip has reappeared in the South, and the inhuman and disgusting spectacle of the chain-gang is beginning to be seen there; that the government of every Southern State is now in the hands of the old slave oligarchy, and that both departments of the National Government soon will be in the same hands; that they believe that when the Government, State and National, shall be in the control of the old masters of the South, they will find means for reducing the freedman to a condition analagous to slavery; that they despair of any change for the better; that everything is waxing worse for the negro in the South, and that the only means of safety is to leave the South.

It must be admitted, if this brief statement of complaints be only half true, that the explanation of the exodus and the justification of the persons composing it are full and ample. The complaints they make against Southern society are such as every man of common honesty and humanity must wish ill-founded; unhappily, however, there is nothing in the nature of these complaints to make them doubtful or surprising. The unjust conduct charged against the late slaveholders is eminently probable. It is an inheritance from the long exercise of irresponsible power by man over man. It is not the natural inferiority of the negro, or the color of his skin. Tyranny is the same proud and selfish thing everywhere, and with all races and colors.

What the negro is now suffering at the hands of his former masters, the white emancipated serfs of Russia are now suffering from the lords and nobles by whom they were formerly held as slaves. In form and appearance the emancipation of the latter was upon better terms than in the case of the negro. The Empire, unlike the Republic, gave her free serfs, or pretended to give them, three acres of land — a start in the world. But the selection and bestowment of this land was unhappily confided to the care of the nobles, their former lords and masters. Thus the lamb was committed to the care of the wolf, and hence the organized assassination now going on in that country; and it will be well for our Southern States if they escape a like fate. The world is slow to learn that no man can wrong his brother without doing a greater wrong to himself. Something may, however, be learned from the lessons of alarm and consternation which are now written all over Russia.

But in contemplating this exodus, it should be kept in mind that the way of an oppressed people from bondage to freedom is never smooth. There is ever in such transition much to overcome on both sides. Neither the master nor the emancipated slave can at once shake off the habits and manners of a long-established past condition. The form may be abolished, but the spirit survives and lingers about the scenes of its former life. The slave brings into the new relation much of the dependence, improvidence and servility of slavery, and the master brings much of his pride, selfishness and love of power. The influence of feudalism has not yet disappeared from Europe. Norman pride is still visible even in England, though centuries have passed since the Saxon was the slave of the Norman; and long years must elapse before all traces of slavery shall disappear from our country. Suffering and hardship made the Saxon strong; and suffering and hardship will make the Anglo-African strong and ultimately successful on the soil of his birth and in the climate to which his color and origin as well as his labor adapt him.

Very evidently there are to be asked and answered many important questions before the friends of humanity can be properly called upon to give their support to this emigration movement. A natural and primary inquiry is: What does it mean? How much ground is it meant to cover? Is the total removal of the whole five millions of colored people from the South contemplated? Or is it proposed to remove only a part? And, if only a part, why a part and not the whole? Is the protection of the rights of the many less important than the same of the few? If the few are to be removed because of the intolerable oppression which prevails in the South, why not the many also? If exodus is good for any, must it not be equally good for all? Then, if the whole five millions are to leave the South, as a doomed country — leave it as Lot left Sodom, or driven out as the Moors were driven out of Spain — then there is a question of ways and means to be considered. Has any definite estimate of the cost of this removal been made? How shall the one or two hundred millions of dollars, which such removal would require, be obtained? Shall it be appropriated by Congress, or voluntarily contributed by the public? Manifestly, with such a debt upon the nation as the war for the Union has created, Congress is not likely to be in a hurry to make any such appropriation. It would much more willingly and readily enact the necessary legislation to protect the freedmen where they are, than appropriate two hundred millions of dollars to help them away to Kansas or elsewhere in the North. The same amount of money and labor required to promote emigration, would, if applied to that end, protect the negro where he is. But suppose, as already suggested, the matter shall not be left at all to Congress, but remitted to the voluntary contributions from the people. Then a swarm of agents must be employed to circulate over the country, hat in hand, soliciting and collecting these contributions, representing to the people everywhere that the cause of the negro is lost in the South, that his only hope and deliverance from a condition of things worse than slavery is removal to Kansas, or to some country outside the Southern States. Then would such an arrangement, such an apostleship of despair be beneficial, or would it be prejudicial to the cause of the freedman? Precisely and plainly, this is a feature of the emigration movement which is open to serious objection.

Voluntary, spontaneous, self-sustained emigration on the part of the freedmen may or may not be commendable. It is a matter with which they alone have to do. The public is not called upon to say or do anything for or against it; but when the public is called upon to take sides, to declare its views, to organize emigration societies, appoint and send out agents to make speeches and collect money to help the freedmen from the South, the public may very properly hesitate. it may not wish to be responsible for the measure, or for the disheartening doctrines by which the measure is supported.

Objection may properly be made upon many grounds. It may well enough be said that the negro question is not so desperate as the advocates of exodus would have the public believe; that there is still reasonable ground of hope that the negro will ultimately have his rights as a man, and be fully protected in the South; that in several of the old slave States his citizenship and his right to vote are already respected and protected; that the same, in time, will be secured for the negro in the other States; that the world was not the work of a day; that even in free New England all the evils generated by slavery did not disappear in a century after the abolition of the system, if, indeed, they have yet entirely disappeared.

Within the last forty years, a dark and shocking picture might be given of the persecution of the negro and his friends, even in the now pre-eminently free State of Massachusetts. It is not more than twenty years ago that Boston supplied a pistol club, if not a rifle club, to break up an abolition meeting, and that one of her most eminent citizens had to be guarded to and from his house, to escape the hand of mobocratic assassins, armed in the interest of slavery. The negro on the Sound between New York and Boston, though a respectable, educated gentleman, was not allowed abaft the wheel, and must sleep, if he slept at all, upon the naked deck, in the open air. Upon no condition, except that of a servant or slave, could he be permitted to go into a cabin. All the handicrafts of New England, too, were closed to him. The appearance of a black man in any workshop or shipyard, as a mechanic, there would have scattered the whole gang of white hands at once. The poor negro was not admitted into the factories to work, or as an apprentice to any trade. He was barber, waiter, whitewasher and wood-sawyer. All of what were considered respectable employments, by a power superior to legal enactments were denied him. But none of these things have moved the negro from New England, and it is well for him that he has remained there. In some respects, Massachusetts was then what the South is now, good missionary ground for anti-slavery writers and speakers. What has been accomplished there, may be accomplished elsewhere.

Bad as is the condition of the negro to-day at the South, there was a time when it was flagrantly and incomparably worse. A few years ago he had nothing — he had not even himself. He belonged to somebody else, who could dispose of his person and his labor as he pleased. Now he has himself, his labor, and his right to dispose of one and the other, as shall best suit his own happiness. He has more. He has a standing in the supreme law of the land, in the Constitution of the United States — not to be changed or affected by any conjunction of circumstances likely to occur in the immediate or remote future. The Fourteenth Amendment makes him a citizen, and the Fifteenth makes him a voter. With power behind him, at work for him, and which cannot be taken from him, the negro of the South may wisely bide his time. The situation at the moment is exceptional and transient. The permanent powers of the Government are all on his side. What though, for the moment, the hand of violence strikes down the negro's rights in the South, those rights will revive, survive and flourish again. They are not the only people who have been in a moment of popular passion maltreated and driven from the polls. The Irish and Dutch have frequently been so treated — Boston, Baltimore and New York have been the scenes of this lawless violence; but those scenes have now disappeared. A Hebrew may even now be rudely repulsed from the door of a hotel; but he will not on that account get up another exodus, as he did three thousand years ago, but will quietly "put money in his purse" and bide his time, knowing that the rising tide of civilization will eventually float him, as it floats all other varieties of the human family to whom floating in any condition is possible.

Of one thing we may be certain, and it is a thing which is destined to be made very prominent not long hence — the negro will either be counted at the polls or not counted in the basis of representation. The South must let the negro vote, or surrender its power in Congress. The chosen horn of this dilemma will finally be to let the negro vote, and vote unmolested. Let us have all the indignant and fiery declamation which the warm hearts of our youthful orators can pour out against Southern meanness, "White Leagues," "Bulldozers," and other "Dark Lantern" organizations; but let us have a little calm, clear reason as well. The latter is a safer guide than the former. On this great question we want light rather than heat, thought rather than feeling, a comprehensive view and appreciation of what the negro has already on his side, as well as of the disadvantages against which he has thus far been compelled to struggle, and still has to struggle.

Without abating one jot of our horror and indignation at the outrages committed in some parts of the Southern States against the negro, we cannot but regard the present agitation of an African exodus from the South as ill-timed, and, in some respects, hurtful. We stand to-day at the beginning of a grand and beneficent reaction. There is a growing recognition of the duty and obligation of the American people to guard, protect and defend the personal and political rights of all the people of all the States; to uphold the principles upon which rebellion was suppressed, slavery abolished, and the country saved from dismemberment and ruin.

We see and feel to-day, as we have not seen and felt before, that the time for conciliation and trusting to the honor of the late rebels and slave-holders has passed. The President of the United States himself, while still liberal, just and generous toward the South, has yet sounded a halt in that direction, and has bravely, firmly and ably asserted the constitutional authority to maintain the public peace in every State in the

Union, and upon every day in the year, and has maintained this ground against all the powers of House and Senate.

We stand at the gateway of a marked and decided change in the statesmanship of our rulers. Every day brings fresh and increasing evidence that we are, and of right ought to be, a Nation; that Confederate notions of the nature and powers of our Government ought to have perished in the rebellion which they supported; that they are anachronisms and superstitions, and no longer fit to be above ground.

National ideas are springing up all around us — the oppressor of the negro is seen to be the enemy of the peace, prosperity and honor of the country.

The attempt to nullify the national Election Laws, to starve the officers where they could not destroy the offices, to attack the national credit when they could not prevent successful resumption, to paralyze the Constitution where they could neither pervert nor set it aside, has all worked against the old slave-holding element, and in the interest of the negro. They have made it evident that the sceptre of political power must soon pass from the party of reaction, revolution, rebellion and slavery to the party of Constitution, liberty and progress. At a time like this, so full of hope and courage, it is unfortunate that a cry of despair should be raised in behalf of the colored people of the South; unfortunate that men are going over the country begging in the name of the poor colored men of the South, and telling the people that the Government has no power to enforce the Constitution and laws in that section, and that there is no hope for the poor negro, but to plant him in the new soil of Kansas and Nebraska.

These men do the colored people of the South a real damage. They give their enemies an advantage in the argument for their manhood and freedom. They assume the inability of the colored people of the South to take care of themselves — the country will be told of the hundreds who go to Kansas, but not of the thousands who stay in Mississippi and Louisiana.

They will be told of the destitute who require material aid, but not of the multitude who are bravely sustaining themselves where they are.

In Georgia the negroes are paying taxes upon six millions of dollars; in Louisiana upon forty or fifty millions; and upon unascertained sums elsewhere in the Southern States.

Why should a people who have made such progress in the course of a few years, now be humiliated and scandalized by exodus agents, begging money to remove them from their homes? especially at a time when every indication favors the position that the wrongs and hardships which they suffer are soon to be redressed.

Besides the objection thus stated, it is manifest that the public and noisy advocacy of a general stampede of the colored people from the South to the North is necessarily an abandonment of the great and paramount principle of protection to person and property in every State of the Union. It is an evasion of a solemn obligation and duty. The business of this nation is to protect its citizens where they are, not to transport them where they will not need protection. The best that can be said of this exodus in this respect is, that it is an attempt to climb up some other than the right way; it is an expedient, a half-way measure, and tends to weaken in the public mind a sense of the absolute right, power and duty of the Government, inasmuch as it concedes, by implication at least, that on the soil of the South the law of the land cannot command obedience, the ballot-box cannot be kept pure, peaceable elections cannot be held, the Constitution cannot be enforced, and the lives and liberties of loyal and peaceable citizens cannot be protected. It is a surrender, a premature, disheartening surrender, since it would secure freedom and free institutions by migration rather than by protection; by flight, rather than by right; by going into a strange land, rather than by staying in one's own. It leaves the whole question of equal rights on the soil of the South open, and still to be settled, with the moral influence of exodus against us, since it is a confession of the utter impracticability of equal rights and equal protection in any State where those rights may be struck down by violence.

It does not appear that the friends of freedom should spend either time or talent in furtherance of this exodus, as a desirable measure, either for the North or the South, for the blacks of the South or the whites of the North. If the people of this country cannot be protected in every State of this Union, the Government of the United States is shorn of its rightful dignity and power, the late rebellion has triumphed, the sovereignty of the nation is an empty name, and the power and authority in individual States is greater than the power and authority of the United States.

Necessity often compels men to migrate, to leave their old homes and seek new ones, to sever old ties and create new ones; but to do this the necessity should be obvious and imperative. It should be a last resort, and only adopted after carefully considering what is against the measure, as well as what is in favor of it. There are prodigal sons everywhere, who are ready to demand the portion of goods that would fall to them, and betake themselves to a strange country. Something is ever lost in the process of migration, and much is sacrificed at home for what is gained abroad. A world of wisdom is in the saying of Mr. Emerson, that "those who made Rome worth going to see, stayed there." Five moves from house to house are said to be worse than a fire. That a rolling stone gathers no moss, has passed into the world's wisdom.

The colored people of the South, just beginning to accumulate a little property, and to lay the foundation of family, should not be in haste to sell that little and be off to the banks of the Mississippi. The habit of roaming from place to place in pursuit of better conditions of existence is by no means a good one. A man should never leave his home for a new one till he has earnestly endeavored to make his immediate surroundings accord with his wishes. The time and energy expended in wandering about from place to place, if employed in making him a comfortable home where he is, will in nine cases out of ten, prove the best investment. No people ever did much for themselves or for the world without the sense and inspiration of native land, of a fixed home, of familiar neighborhood and common associations. The fact of being to the manor born has an elevating power upon the mind and heart of a man. It is a more cheerful thing to be able to say: I was born here, and know all the people, than to say: I am a stranger here, and know none of the people.

It cannot be doubted that in so far as this exodus tends to promote restlessness in the colored people of the South, to unsettle their feeling of home and to sacrifice positive advantages where they are for fancied ones in Kansas or elsewhere, it is an evil. Some have sold their little homes, their chickens, mules and pigs, at a sacrifice, to follow the exodus. Let it be understood that you are going, and you advertise the fact that your mule has lost half his value — for your staying with him makes half his value. Let the colored people of Georgia offer their six millions' worth of property for sale, with the purpose to leave Georgia, and they will not realize half its value. Land is not worth much where there are no people to occupy it, and a mule is not worth much where there is no one to drive him.

It may safely be asserted that, whether advocated and commended to favor on the ground that it will increase the political power of the Republican party, and thus help to make a solid North against a solid South; or upon the ground that it will increase the power and influence of the colored people as a political element, and enable them the better to protect their rights, and insure their moral and social elevation, the exodus will prove a disappointment, a mistake and a failure; because, as to strengthening the Republican party, the emigrants will go only to those States where the Republican party is strong and solid enough already without their votes; and in respect to the other part of the argument, it will fail because it takes colored voters from a section of the country where they are sufficiently numerous to elect some of their number to places of honor and profit, and places them in a country where their proportion to other classes will be so small as not to be recognized as a political element, or entitled to be represented by one of themselves. And, further, because, go where they will, they must for a time inevitably carry with them poverty, ignorance and other repulsive incidents, inherited from their former condition as slaves — a circumstance which is about as likely to make votes for Democrats as for Republicans, and to raise up bitter prejudices against them as to raise up friends for them.

No people can be much respected in this country, where all are eligible to office, that cannot point to any one of their class in an honorable, responsible position. In sending a few men to Congress, the negroes of the South have done much to dispel prejudice and raise themselves in the estimation of the country and the world. By staying where they are, they may be able to send abler, better and more effective representatives of their race to Congress than it was possible for them to send at first, because of their want of education and their recent liberation from bondage. In the South the negro has at least the possibility of power, in the North he has no such possibility; and it is for him to say how well he can afford to part with this possible power.

But another argument in favor of this emigration is, that having a numerical superiority in Mississippi, Louisiana and South Carolina, and thereby possessing the ability to choose some of their own number to represent them in the State and Nation, they are necessarily brought into antagonism with the white race, and invite the very political persecution of which they complain. So they are told that the best remedy for this persecution is to surrender the right and advantage given them by the Constitution and the Government of electing men of color to office. They are not to overcome prejudice and persecution where it is, but to go where it is not; not to stand where they are, and demand the full Constitutional protection which the Government is solemnly bound to give, but to go where the protection of the Government is not needed. Plainly enough, this is an evasion of a solemn obligation and duty; an attempt to climb up some other way, a half-way measure, a makeshift, a miserable substitution of expediency for right. For an egg, it gives the negro a stone.

The dissemination of this doctrine by the agents of emigration cannot but do the cause of equal rights much harm. It lets the public mind down from the high ground of a great national duty to a miserable compromise, in which wrong surrenders nothing, and right everything. The South is not to repent its crimes and submit to the Constitution, in common with all other parts of the country, but such repentance and submission is to be conveniently made unnecessary by removing the temptation to commit violations of the law and the Constitution. Men may be pardoned for refusing their assent to a measure supported upon a principle so unsound, subversive and pernicious. The Nation should be held steadily to the high and paramount principle that allegiance and protection are inseparable, that this Government is solemnly bound to protect and defend the lives and liberties of all its citizens, of whatever race or color, or of whatever political or religious opinion, and to do this in every State and Territory within the American Union.

Then, again, is there to be no stopping-place for the negro? Suppose that, by-and-by, some "Sand-lot orator" shall arise in Kansas, as in California, and take it into his head to stir up the mob against the negro, as he stirred up the mob against the Chinese? What then? Must the negro have another exodus? Does not one exodus invite another? and in advocating one, do we not sustain the demand for another?

Plainly enough, the exodus is less harmful as a measure, than are the arguments by which it is supported. The one is the result of a feeling of outrage and despair; but the other comes of cool, selfish calculation. One is the result of honest despair, and appeals powerfully to the sympathies of men; the other is an appeal to our selfishness, which shrinks from doing right because the way is difficult.

Not only is the South the best locality for the negro, on the ground of his political powers and possibilities, but it is best for him as a field of labor. He is there, as he is nowhere else, an absolute necessity. He has a monopoly of the labor market. His labor is the only labor which can successfully offer itself for sale in that market. This fact, with a little wisdom and firmness, will enable him to sell his labor there, on terms more favorable to himself than he can elsewhere. As there are no competitors or substitutes, he can demand living prices with the certainty that the demand will be complied with. Exodus would deprive him of this advantage. It would take him from a country where the landowners and planters must have his labor, or allow their fields to go untilled and their purses unsupplied with cash, to a country where the landowners are able and proud to do their own work, and do not need to hire hands, except for limited periods, at certain seasons of the year. The effect of this will be to send the negro to the towns and cities to compete with white labor. With what result, let the past tell. They will be crowded into lanes and alleys, cellars and garrets, poorly provided with the necessaries of life, and will gradually die out.

The negro, as already intimated, is pre-eminently a Southern man. He is so both in constitution and habits, in body as well as mind. He will not only take with him to the North Southern modes of labor, but Southern modes of life. The careless and improvident habits of the South cannot be set aside in a generation. If they are adhered to in the North, in the fierce winds and snows of Kansas and Nebraska, the emigration must be large to keep up their numbers.

It would appear, therefore, that neither the laws of politics, labor nor climate favor this exodus. It does not conform to the laws of healthy emigration, which proceeds not from south to north, not from heat to cold, but from east to west, and in climates to which the emigrants are more or less adapted and accustomed.

As an assertion of power by a people hitherto held in bitter contempt; as an emphatic and stinging protest against highhanded, greedy and shameless injustice to the weak and defenseless; as a means of opening the blind eyes of oppressors to their folly and peril, the exodus has done valuable service. Whether it has accomplished all of which it is capable in this particular direction, for the present, is a question which may well be considered. With a moderate degree of intelligent leadership among the laboring class at the South, properly handling the justice of their cause, and wisely using the exodus example, they can easily exact better terms for their labor than ever before. Exodus is medicine, not food; it is for disease, not health — it is not to be taken from choice, but necessity. In anything like a normal condition of things, the South is the best place for the negro. Nowhere else is there for him a promise of a happier future. Let him stay there if he can, and save both the South and himself to civilization. While, however, it may be the highest wisdom in the circumstances for the freedmen to stay where they are, no encouragement should be given to any measures of coercion to keep them there. The American people are bound, if they are or can be bound to anything, to keep the North gate of the South open to black and white, and to all the people. The time to assert a right, Webster says, is, when it is called in question. If it is attempted by force or fraud to compel the colored people to stay there, they should by all means go — go quickly, and die, if need be, in the attempt.

Thus far, and to this extent, any man may be an emigrationist; and thus far, and to this extent, I certainly am an emigrationist. In no case must the negro be "bottled up" or "caged up." He must be left free, like every other American citizen, to choose his own local habitation, and to go where he shall like. Though it may not be for his interest to leave the South, his right and power to leave it may be the best means of making it possible for him to stay there in peace.

Woe to the oppressed and destitute of all countries and races, if the rich and powerful are to decide when and where they shall go or stay! The deserving hired man gets his wages increased when he can tell his employer that he can get better wages elsewhere. And when all hope is gone from the hearts of the laboring classes of the Old World, they can come across the sea to the New. If they could not do that, their crushed hearts would break under increasing burdens. The right to emigrate is one of the most useful and precious of all rights.

But not only to the oppressed, but to the oppressor, is the free use of this right necessary. To attempt to keep the freedmen in the South — those who are spirited enough to undertake the risks and hardships of emigration — would involve great possible danger to all concerned. Ignorant and cowardly as the negro may be, he has been known to fight bravely for his liberty. He went down to Harper's Ferry with John Brown, and fought as bravely and died as nobly as any. There have been Nathaniel Turners and Denmark Veseys among them in the United States; Joseph Cinquees, Madison Washingtons and Tillmons on the sea, and Toussaint l'Ouvertures on land. Even his enemies, during the late war, had to confess that the negro is a good fighter, when once in a fight. If he runs, it is only as all men will run when they are whipped. This is no time to trifle with the rights of men. All Europe to-day is studded with the material for a wild conflagration. Every day brings us news of plots and conspiracies against oppressive power.

An able writer in the North American Review for July, himself a Nihilist, in a powerful article defends the extremest measures of his party, and shows that the treatment of the emancipated peasants by the Government and landed aristocracy of Russia is very similar to that now practiced toward the freedmen by the landed aristocracy of the South. Like causes will produce like effects the world over. It will not be wise for the Southern slave-holders and their successors to shape their policy upon the presumption that the negro's cowardice or forbearance has no limit. The fever of freedom is already in the negro's blood. He is not just what he was fourteen years ago. To forcibly dam up the stream of emigration would be a measure of extreme madness, as well as oppression. It would be exposing the heart of the oppressor to the pistol and dagger, and his home to fire and pillage. The cry of "Land and Liberty," the watchword of the Nihilistic party in Russia, has a music in it sweet to the ear of all oppressed peoples; and well shall it be for the land-holders of the South if they shall learn wisdom in time, and adopt such a course of just treatment toward the landless laborers of the South in the future as shall make this popular watchword uncontagious and unknown among them, and further stampedes to the North wholly unknown, undesirable and impossible.

Unconstitutionality of Slavery

Lecture Delivered in Glasgow, Scotland 26 March 1860

I have witnessed with great pleasure the growing interest in the great question of slavery in this city, and in Scotland generally. Meetings with reference to that question have become more abundant of late than perhaps at any time since the abolition of slavery in the British West Indies.

I read with deep interest the speeches made recently at a meeting called to sympathise with and to assist that faithful champion of the cause of my enslaved fellow-countrymen, Dr. Cheever.

I have also read of another meeting in your city, having reference to the improvement and elevation of the people of Africa—having reference to the cultivation of cotton and the opening up of commerce between this and that land. All these movements are in the right direction. I accept them and hail them as signs of "the good time coming," when Ethiopia "shall stretch out her hands to God" in deed and in truth.

There have been, also, other meetings in your city since it was my privilege last to address you. I have read with much care a speech recently delivered in the City Hall. It is published in one of your most respectable journals.

The minuteness and general shading of that report convince me that the orator= was his own reporter. At any rate, there is but little evidence= or few marks of its having been tampered with by any than one exceedingly friendly to the sentiments it contains.

On some accounts I read that speech with regret; on others with much satisfaction.

I was certainly pleased with the evidence it afforded that the orator has largely recovered his long-lost health, and much of his wonted eloquence and fire; but my chief ground of satisfaction is that its delivery—perhaps I ought to say its publication—for I would not have noticed the speech had it not been published in just such a journal as that in which it was published—furnishes an occasion for bringing before the friends of my enslaved people one phase of the great struggle going on between liberty and slavery in the United States which I deem important, and which I think, before I get through, my audience will agree with me is a very important phase of that struggle.

The North British Mail honored me with a few pointed remarks in dissent from certain views held by me on another occasion in this city; but as it rendered my speech on that occasion very fairly to the public, I did not feel at all called upon to reply to its strictures.

The case is different now. I am brought face to face with two powers. I stand before you under the fire of both platform and press. Not to speak, under the circumstances, would subject me and would subject my cause to misconstruction. You might be led to suppose that I had no reasons for the ground that I occupied here when I spoke in another place before you.

Let me invite your attention, I may say your indulgent attention, to this very interesting phase of the question of slavery in the United States.

My assailant, as he had a perfect right to do—that is, if he felt that that was the best possible service he could do to the cause of American slavery—under advertisement to deliver an "anti-slavery lecture"—a lecture on the present aspect of the anti-slavery movement in America—treated the citizens of Glasgow to an "anti-Douglass" lecture.

He seemed to feel that to discredit me was an important work, and therefore he came up to that work with all his wonted power and eloquence, proving himself to be just as powerful and skillful a debater, in all its arts, high and low, as long practice, as constant experience could well fit a man to be.

I award to the eloquent lecturer, as I am sure you do, all praise for his skill and ability, and fully acknowledge his many valuable services, in other days, to the anti-slavery cause both in England and America. We all remember how nobly he confronted the Borthwicks and the Breckenridges in other days, and vanquished them. These victories are safe; they are not to be forgotten. They belong to his past, and will render his name dear and glorious to aftercoming generations. He then enjoyed the confidence of many of the most illustrious philanthropists that Scotland has ever raised up. He had at his back, at those times, the Wardlaws, the Kings, the Heughs, and Robsons——men who are known the world over for their philanthropy, for their Christian benevolence.

He was strong in those days, for he stood before the people of Scotland as the advocate of a great and glorious cause ——he stood up for the dumb, for the down-trodden, for the outcasts of the earth, and not for a mere party, not for the mere sect whose mischievous and outrageous opinions he now consents to advocate in your hearing.

When in Glasgow a few weeks ago, I embraced the occasion to make a broad statement concerning the various plans proposed for the abolition of slavery in the United States, but I very frankly stated with what I agreed and from what I differed; but I did so, I trust, in a spirit of fair dealing, of candor, and not in a miserable, man-worshipping, and mutual-admiration spirit, which can do justice only to the party with which it may happen to go for the moment.

One word further. No difference of opinion, no temporary alienations, no personal assaults shall ever lead me to forget that some who, in America, have often made me the subject of personal abuse, are at the same time, in their own way, earnestly working for the abolition of slavery.

They are men who thoroughly understand the principle, that they who are not for us, are against us, but who unfortunately have failed to learn that they who are not against us are on our part in regard to the speaker to whom I am referring, and who by the way is, perhaps the least vindictive of his party, I shall say that I cannot praise his speech, for it is needlessly, or was needlessly personal calling me by name over, I think, fifty times, and dealing out blows upon me as if I had been savagely attacking him.

In character and manliness that speech was not only deficient, I think, but most shamefully one-sided; and while it was remarkably plausible, and well calculated to catch the popular ear, which could not well discriminate between what was fact and what was fiction in regard to the subject then discussed, I do not hesitate to pronounce that speech false in statement, false in its assumptions, false in its inferences, false in its quotations even, and in its arguments, and false in all its leading conclusions.

On very many accounts, he who stands before a British audience to denounce any thing peculiarly American in connection with slavery has a very marked and decided advantage. It is not hard to believe the very worst of any country where a system like slavery has existed for centuries.

This feeling towards America, and towards every thing American, is very natural and very useful.

I refer to it now not to condemn it; but to remind you that it is just possible that this feeling may be carried to too great a length. It may be that this feeling may be too active, and lead the people of Great Britain to accept as true some things concerning America which are utterly false, and to reject as false some other things which are entirely true.

My assailant largely took advantage of this noble British feeling in denouncing the constitution and Union of America. He knew how deep and intense was your hatred of slavery. He knew the strength of that feeling, and the noble uses to which it might have been directed.

I know it also, but I would despise myself if I could be guilty of taking advantage of such a sentiment, and making it the means of propagating error, falsehood, and prejudice against any institution or against any class of men in the United States. I am willing that these words shall be regarded as marked words.

I have often felt how easy it would be, if one were so disposed, to make false representations of things as they are in America; to disparage whatever of good might exist there, or shall exist there, and to exaggerate whatever is bad in that country.

I intend to show that this very thing was done by the speaker to whom I have referred; that his speech was calculated to convey impressions and ideas totally, grossly, outrageously at variance with truth concerning the constitution and Union of the American States.

You will think this very strong language. I think so too; and it becomes me to look well to myself in using such language, for if I fail to make out my case, I am sure there are parties not a few who will see that fair play is done on the other side.

But I have no fear at all of inability to justify what I have said; and if any friend of mine was led to doubt, from the confident manner in which I was assailed, I beg that such doubt may now be put aside until, at least, I have been heard. I will make good, I promise you, my entire characterisation of that speech.

Reading speeches is not my forte, and you will bear with me until I get my harness on. I have fully examined my ground, and while I own myself nothing in comparison with my assailant in point of ability, I have no manner of doubt as to the rectitude of the position I occupy on the question.

Now, what is that question? Much will be gained at the outset if you fully and clearly understand the real question under discussion—the question and difference between us.

Indeed, nothing can be understood till this is understood. Things are often confounded and treated as the same for no better reason than that they seem alike or look alike, and this is done even when in their nature and character they are totally distinct, totally separate, and even opposed to each other. This jumbling up of things is a sort of dust-throwing which is often indulged in by small men who argue for victory rather than for truth.

Thus, for instance, the American government and the American constitution are often spoken of in the speech to which I refer as being synonymous—as one and the same thing; whereas, in point of fact, they are entirely distinct from each other and totally different.

In regard to the question of slavery, certainly they are different from each other; they are as distinct from each other as the compass is from the ship—as distinct from each other as the chart is from the course which a vessel may be sometimes steering. They are not one and the same thing.

If the American government has been mean, sordid, mischievous, devilish, it is no proof whatever that the constitution of government has been the same.

And yet, in the speech to which some of you listened, these sins of the government or administration of the government were charged directly upon the constitution and Union of the states.

What, then, is the question? I will state what it is not. It is not whether slavery existed in the United States at the time of the adoption of the constitution; It is not whether slaveholders took part in framing the constitution of the United States; it is not whether these slaveholders in their hearts intended to secure certain advantages for slavery in the constitution of the United States; it is not whether the American government has been wielded during seventy-two years on behalf of slavery; it is not whether a pro-slavery interpretation has been put upon the constitution in American courts —all these points may be true or they may be false, they may be accepted or they may be rejected, without at all affecting the question at issue between myself and the "City Hall."

The real question between the parties differing at this point in America may be fairly stated thus:—"Does the United States constitution guarantee to any class or description of people in that country the right to enslave or hold as property any other class or description of people in that country?"

The second question is:—"Is the dissolution of the Union between the Slave States and the Free States required by fidelity to the slaves or the just demands of conscience;?" Or, in other words, "Is the refusal to exercise the elective franchise or to hold office in America, the surest, wisest, and best mode of acting for the abolition of slavery in that country?"

To these questions the Garrisonians in America answer, "Yes." They hold that the constitution is a slave-holding instrument, and will not cast a vote, or hold office under it, and denounce all who do vote or hold office under it as pro-slavery men, though they may be in their hearts and in their actions as far from being slaveholders as are the poles of the moral universe apart. I, on the other hand, deny that the constitution guarantees the right to hold property in men, and believe that the way, the true way, to abolish slavery in America is to vote such men into power as will exert their moral and political influence for the abolition of slavery.

This is the issue plainly stated, and you shall judge between us.

Before we examine into the disposition, tendency, and character of the constitution of the United States, I think we had better ascertain what the constitution itself is. Before looking at what it means, let us see what it is.

For here, too, there has been endless dust-throwing on the part of those opposed to office.

What is the constitution? It is no vague, indefinite, floating, unsubstantial something, called, according to any man's fancy, now a weasel and now a whale. But it is something substantial.

It is a plainly written document; not in Hebrew nor in Greek, but in English, beginning with a preamble, fitted out with articles, sections, provisions, and clauses, defining the rights, powers, and duties to be secured, claimed, and exercised under its authority.

It is not even like the British constitution. It is not made up of enactments of parliament, decisions of courts, and the established usages of the government.

The American constitution is a written instrument, full and complete in itself.

No court, no congress, no legislature, no combination in the country can add one word to it, or take one word from it..

It is a thing in itself; complete in itself; has a character of its own; and it is important that this should be kept in mind as I go on with the discussion.

It is a great national enactment, done by the people, and can only be altered, amended, or changed in anyway, shape, or form by the people who enacted it.

I am careful to make this statement here; in America it would not be necessary. It would not be necessary here if my assailant had shown that he had as sincere and earnest a desire to set before you the simple truth, as he has shown to vindicate his particular sect in America.

Again, it should be borne in mind that the mere text of that constitution—the text and only the text, and not any commentaries or creeds written upon the text—is the constitution of the United States.

It should also be borne in mind that the intentions of those who framed the constitution, be they good or bad, be they for slavery or against slavery, are to be respected so far, and so far only, as they have succeeded in getting these intentions expressed in the written instrument itself. This is also important.

It would be the wildest of absurdities, and would lead to the most endless confusions and mischiefs, if, instead of looking to the written instrument itself for its meaning, it were attempted to make us go in search of what could be the secret motives and dishonest intentions of some of the men who might have taken part in writing or adopting it.

It was what they said that was adopted by the people; not what they were ashamed or afraid to say, or really omitted to say.

It was not what they tried, nor what they concealed; it was what they wrote down, not what they kept back, that the people adopted.

It was only what was declared upon its face that was adopted—not their secret understandings, if there were any such understandings.

Bear in mind, also, and the fact is an important one, that the framers of the constitution, the men who wrote the constitution, sat with closed doors in the city of Philadelphia while they wrote it. They sat with closed doors, and this was done purposely, that nothing but the result, the pure result of their labours should be seen, and that that result might stand alone and be judged of on its own merits, and adopted on its own merits, without any influence being exerted upon them by the debates.

It should also be borne in mind, and the fact is still more important, that the debates in the convention that framed the constitution of the United States, and by means of which a pro-slavery interpretation is now attempted to be forced upon that instrument, were not published until nearly thirty years after the constitution of the United States; so that the men who adopted the constitution could not be supposed to understand the secret underhand intentions that might have controlled the actions of the convention in making it.

These debates were purposely kept out of view, in order that the people might not adopt the secret motives, the unexpressed intentions of anybody, but simply the text of the paper itself.

These debates form no part of the original agreement, and, therefore, are entitled to no respect or consideration in discussing what is the character of the constitution of the United States.

I repeat, the paper itself and only the paper itself, with its own plainly written purposes, is the constitution of the United States, and it must stand or fall, flourish or fade, on its own individual and self-declared purpose and object.

Again, where would be the advantage of a written constitution, I pray you, if, after we have it written, instead of looking to its plain, common sense reading, we should go in search of its meaning to the secret intentions of the individuals who may have had something to do with writing the paper?

What will the people of America a hundred years hence, care about the intentions of the men who framed the constitution of the United States? These men were for a day—for a generation, but the constitution is for ages; and, a hundred years hence, the very names of the men who took part in framing that instrument will, perhaps, be blotted out or forgotten.

Whatever we may owe to the framers of the constitution, we certainly owe this to ourselves, and to mankind, and to God, that we maintain the truth of our own language, and do not allow villainy, not even the villainy of slaveholding—which, as John Wesley says, is the sum of all villainies—to clothe itself in the garb of virtuous language, and get itself passed off as a virtuous thing, in consequence of that language.

We owe it to ourselves to compel the devil to wear his own garments; particularly in law we owe it to ourselves to compel wicked legislators, when they undertake a malignant purpose in innocent and benevolent language, we owe it to ourselves that we circumvent their wicked designs to this extent, that if they want to put it to a bad purpose, we will put it to a good purpose.

Common sense, common justice, and sound rules of interpretation all drive us to the words of the law for the meaning of the law.

The practice of the American government is dwelt upon with much fervour as conclusive as to the slaveholding character of the American constitution. This is really the strong point, and the only strong point, made in the speech in the City Hall; but, good as this argument is, it is not conclusive.

A wise man has said that few people are found better than their laws, but many have been found worse; and the American people are no exception to this rule. I think it will be found they are much worse than their laws, particularly their constitutional laws.

It is just possible the people's practice may be diametrically opposed to their own declared, their own acknowledged laws, and their own acknowledged principles.

Our blessed Saviour when upon earth found the traditions of men taking the place of the law and the prophets. The Jews asked him why his disciples ate with unwashed hands, and he brought them to their senses by telling them that they had made void the law by their traditions.

Moses, on account of the hardness of the hearts of men, allowed the Jews to put away their wives; but it was not so at the beginning.

The American people, likewise, have made void their law by their traditions; they have trampled upon their own constitution, stepped beyond the limits set for themselves, and, in their ever-abounding iniquity, established a constitution of action outside of the fundamental law of the land.

While the one is good, the other is evil; while the one is for liberty, the other is in favour of slavery; the practice of the American government is one thing, and the character of the constitution of the government is quite another and different thing.

After all, Mr. Chairman, the fact that my opponent thought it necessary to go outside of the constitution to prove it pro-slavery, whether that going out is to the practice of the government, or to the secret intentions of the writers of the paper itself, the fact that men do go out is very significant.

It is an admission that the thing they look for is not to be found where only it ought to be found if found at all, and that is, in the written constitution itself.

If it is not there, it is nothing to the purpose if it is found any where else; but I shall have more to say on this point hereafter.

The very eloquent lecturer at the City Hall doubtless felt some embarrassment from the fact that he had literally to give the constitution a pro-slavery interpretation; because on its very face it conveys an entirely opposite meaning. He thus sums up what he calls the slaveholding provisions of the constitution, and I quote his words:—

"Article 1, section 9, provides for the continuance of the African slave-trade for twenty years after the adoption of the constitution.

"Article 4, section 2, provides for the recovery from other States of fugitive slaves.

"Article 1, section 2, gives the slave States a representation of three-fifths of all the slave population; and

"Article 1, section 8, requires the President to use the military, naval, ordnance, and militia resources of the entire country for the suppression of slave insurrections, in the same manner as he would employ them to repel invasion."

Now, Mr. President, and ladies and gentlemen, any man reading this statement, or hearing it made with such a show of exactness, would unquestionably suppose that the speaker or writer had given the plain written text of the constitution itself.

I can hardly believe that that gentleman intended to make any such impression on his audience, and yet what are we to make of it, this circumstantial statement of the provisions of the constitution? How can we regard it?

How can he be screened from the charge of having perpetrated a deliberate and point blank misrepresentation?

That individual has seen fit to place himself before the public as my opponent.

Well, ladies and gentlemen, if he had placed himself before the country as an enemy, I could not have desired him—even an enemy—to have placed himself in a position so false, and to have committed himself to statements so grossly at variance with the truth as those statements I have just read from him.

Why did he not read the constitution to you? Why did he read that which was not the constitution-—for I contend he did read that which was not the constitution.

He pretended to be giving you chapter and verse, section and clause, paragraph and provision, and yet he did not give you a single clause or single paragraph of that constitution.

Ed Note: Apparent Audience Reaction of Disbelief.

You can hardly believe it, but I will make good what I say, that, though reading to you article upon article, as you supposed while listening to him, he did not read a word from the constitution of the United States; not one word.

(Applause)

You had better not applaud until you hear the other side and what are the real words of the constitution.

Why did he not give you the plain words of the constitution? He can read; he had the constitution before him; he had there chapter and verse, the places where those things he alleged to be found in the constitution were to be found.

Why did he not read them? Oh, Sir, I fear that that gentleman knows too well why he did not.

I happen to know that there are no such words in the American constitution as "African slave-trade," no such words as "slave-representation," no such words as "fugitive slaves," no such words as "slave insurrections" anywhere to be found in that constitution.

You can hardly think a man would stand up before an audience of people in Glasgow, and make a statement so circumstantial, with every mark of particularity, to point out to be in the constitution what is not there.

You shall see a slight difference in my manner of treating that subject and that which my opponent has thought fit, for reasons satisfactory to himself, to pursue.

What he withheld, that I will spread before you; what he suppressed, I will bring to light; and what he passed over in silence, I will proclaim.

Here then are the several provisions of the constitution to which reference has been made. I will read them word for word, just as they stand in the paper, in the constitution itself.

Article 1, section 2, declares that representations and direct taxes shall be apportioned among the several States which may be included within this Union, according to their respective numbers, which shall be determined by adding to the whole number of free persons, including those bound to service for a term of years, excluding Indians not taxed, three-fifths of all other persons.

Article 1, section 9.—The migration or importation of any such persons as any of the States now existing may think fit to admit shall not be prohibited the Congress prior to the year 1808, but a tax or duty may be imposed on such importation not exceeding ten dollars for each person.

Article 4.—No person held to service or labour in one state under the laws thereof escaping to another shall, in consequence of any law or regulation therein, be discharged from such service or labour, but shall be delivered up on claim of the party to whom such service or labour may be due.

Article 1, section 8.—To provide for calling out the militia to execute the laws of the Union, suppress insurrections, and repel invasions.

Here then are the provisions of the constitution which the most extravagant defenders of slavery have ever claimed to guarantee the right of property in man.

These are the provisions which have been pressed into the service of the human fleshmongers of America; let us look at them just as they stand, one by one.

You will notice there is not a word said there about "slave-trade," not a word said there about "slave insurrections;" not a word there about "three-fifths representation of slaves;" not a word there which any man outside of America, and who had not been accustomed to claim these particular provisions of the Constitution, would ever suspect had the remotest reference to slavery.

I deny utterly that these provisions of these constitution guarantee, or were intended to guarantee, in any shape or form, the right of property in man in the United States.

But let us grant, for the sake of argument, that the first of these provisions, referring to the basis of representation and taxation, does refer to slaves.

We are not compelled to make this admission, for it might fairly apply, and indeed was intended to apply, to aliens and others, living in the United State, but who were not naturalised.

But giving the provision the very worst construction—that it applies to slaves—what does it amount to?

I answer—and see you bear it in mind, for it shows the disposition of the constitution to slavery—I take the very worst aspect, and admit all that is claimed or that can be admitted consistently with truth; and I answer that this very provision, supposing it refers to slaves, is in itself a downright disability imposed upon the slave system of America, one which deprives the slaveholding States of at least two-fifths of their natural basis of representation.

A black man in a free State is worth just two-fifths more than a black man in a slave State, as a basis of political power under the constitution.

Therefore, instead of encouraging slavery, the constitution encourages freedom, by holding out to every slaveholding State the inducement of an increase of two-fifths of political power by becoming a free State.

So much for the three-fifths clause; taking it at its worst, it still leans to freedom, not to slavery; for be it remembered that, the constitution nowhere forbids a black man to vote. No "white," no "black," no "slaves," no "slaveholder"—nowhere in the instrument are any of these words to bo found,

I come to the next, that which it is said guarantees the continuance of the African slave-trade for twenty years. I will also take that for just what my opponent alleges it to have been, although the constitution does not warrant any such conclusion.

But, to be liberal, let us suppose it did, and what follows?

Why, this—that this part of the constitution of the United States expired by its own limitation no fewer than fifty two years ago. My opponent is just fifty-two years too late in seeking the dissolution of the Union on account of this clause, for it expired as far back as 1808.

He might as well attempt to break down the British parliament and break down the British constitution, because, three hundred years ago, Queen Elizabeth granted to Sir John Hawkins the right to import Africans into the colonies in the West Indies. This ended some three hundred years ago; ours ended only fifty-two years ago, and I ask is the constitution of the United States to be condemned to everlasting infamy because of what was done fifty-two years ago?

But there is still more to be said about this provision of the constitution.

At the time the constitution was adopted, the slave trade was regarded as the jugular vein of slavery itself, and it was thought that slavery would die with the death of the slave trade.

No less philanthropic, no less clear-sighted men than your Wilberforce and Clarkson supposed that the abolition of the slave-trade would be the abolition of slavery. Their theory was—cut off the stream, and of course the pond or lake would dry up: cut off the stream flowing out from Africa, and the slave-trade in America and the colonies would perish.

The fathers who framed the American constitution supposed that in making provision for the abolition of the African slave-trade they were making provision for the abolition of slavery itself, and they incorporated this clause in the constitution, not to perpetuate the traffic in human flesh, but to bring that unnatural traffic to an end.

Outside of the Union the slave-trade could be carried on to an indefinite period; but the men who framed the constitution, and who proposed its adoption, said to the slave States,—If you would purchase the privileges of this Union, you must consent that the humanity of this nation shall lay its hand upon this traffic at least in twenty years after the adoption of the constitution. So much for the African slave-trade clause.

Mark you, it does not say one word about the African slave-trade. Secondly, if it does, it expired by its own limitation more than fifty years ago. Thirdly, the constitution is anti-slavery, because it looked to the abolition of slavery rather than to its perpetuity. Fourthly, it showed that the intentions of the framers of the constitution were good, not bad.

If if you can't get a man to take the pledge that he will stop drinking liquor today, it is something if you will get him to promise to take it tomorrow, and if the men who made the American constitution did not bring the African slave-trade to an end instantly, it was something to succeed in bringing it to an end in twenty years.

I now go to the slave insurrection clause, though, in truth, there is no such clause in the constitution. But, suppose that this clause in the constitution refers to the abolition or rather the suppression of slave insurrections; suppose we admit that congress has a right to call out the army and navy to quell insurrections, and to repel any efforts on the part of the slaves to gain their freedom—to put down violence of any sort, and slave violence in particular—what follows?

I hold that the right to suppress an insurrection carries with it also the right to determine by what means the insurrection shall be suppressed; and, under an anti-slavery administration, were your humble servant in the presidential chair of the United States, which in all likelihood never will be the case, and were an insurrection to break out in the southern states among the slave inhabitants, what would I do in the circumstance, I would suppress the insurrection, and I should choose my own way of suppressing it; I should have the right, under the constitution, to my own manner of doing it.

If I could make out, as I believe I could, that slavery is itself an insurrection—that it is an insurrection by one party in the country against the just rights of another part of the people in the country, a constant invitation to insurrection, a constant source of danger—as the executive officer of the United States it would be my duty not only to put down the insurrection, but to put down the cause of the insurrection.

I would have no hesitation at all in supporting the constitution of the United States in consequence of its provisions. The constitution should be obeyed, should be rightly obeyed. We should say to the slaves, and we should say to their masters,

"We see that a forced system of labour endangers the peace that we are sworn to protect, and we now put it away, and leave you to pay honest wages for honest work."

In a word, with regard to putting down insurrection, I would just write a proclamation, and the proclamation would be based upon the old prophetic model of proclaiming liberty throughout all the land, to all the inhabitants thereof.

But there is one other provision called the "Fugitive Slave Provision." It is called so by those who wish it to subserve the interests of slavery.

"Let us go back," says the City Hall, "to 1787, and enter Liberty Hall, Philadelphia, where sat in convention the illustrious men"—very illustrious! if they were the scamps and scoundrels he would make them out to be—"who framed the constitution—with George Washington in the chair.

"On the 27th of September, Mr. Butler and Mr. Pinckney, two delegates from the state of South Carolina, moved that the constitution should require fugitive slaves and servants to be delivered up like criminals, and after a discussion on the subject, the clause as it stands in the constitution was adopted.

"After this, in conventions held in the several States to ratify the constitution, the same meaning was attached to the words.

"For example, Mr. Madison, (afterwards President) in recommending the, constitution to his constituents, told them that this clause would secure them their property in slaves."

I must ask you to look well to the statement.

Upon its face it would seem to be a full and fair disclosure of the real transaction it professes to describe; and yet I declare unto you, knowing as I do the facts in the case, that I am utterly amazed, utterly amazed at the downright untruth which that very simple, plain statement really conveys to you about that transaction.

I dislike to use this very strong language, but you shall see that the case is quite as strong as the language employed.

Under these fair-seeming words now quoted, I say there is downright untruth conveyed. The man who could make such a statement may have all the craftiness of a lawyer, but I think he will get but very little credit for the candour of a Christian.

What could more completely destroy all confidence than the making of such a statement as that!

The case which he describes is entirely different from the real case as transacted at the time.

Mr. Butler and Mr. Pinckney did indeed bring forward a proposition after the convention had framed the constitution, a proposition for the return of fugitive slaves to their masters precisely as criminals are returned.

And what happened?

Mr. Thompson—oh! I beg pardon for calling his name—tells you that after a debate it was withdrawn, and the proposition as it stands in the constitution was adopted.

He does not tell you what was the nature of the debate. Not one word of it. No; it would not have suited his purpose to have done that. It would have been against his side of the question to have done that.

I will tell you what was the purport of that debate.

After debate and discussion the provision as it stands was adopted. The purport of the provisions as brought forward by Mr. Butler and Mr. Pinckney was this:

"No person called to servitude in any State under the laws thereof, escaping into another, shall, in consequence of any law or regulation therein, be discharged from such service and labour, but shall be delivered up on claim, and passed to whom such service or labour may be due."

Very well, what happened?

The proposition was met by a storm of opposition in the convention; members rose up in all directions saying that they had no more business to catch slaves for their masters than they had to catch horses for their owners—that they would not undertake any such thing,

and the convention instructed a committee to alter that provision and the word "servitude," so that it might apply not to slaves, but to freemen—to persons bound to serve and labour, and not to slaves.

And thus far it seems that Mr. Madison, who was quoted so triumphantly, tells us in these very Madison Papers that that word was struck out from the constitution, because it applied to slaves and not to freemen, and that the convention refused to have that word in the constitution, simply because they did not wish, and would not have the idea that there could be property in men in that instrument.

These are Madison's own words, so that he can be quoted on both sides.

But it may be asked, if the clause does not apply to slaves, to whom does it apply? It says—

"No person serving and labouring escaping to another State shall be discharged from such service or labour, but shall be delivered up to whom such service or labour may be due."

To whom does it apply if not to slaves?

I answer that it applied at the time of its adoption to a very numerous class of persons in America; and I have the authority of no less a person than Daniel Webster that it was intended to apply to that class of men—a class of persons known in America as "Redemptioners."

There was quite a number of them at that day, who had been taken to America precisely as coolies have been taken to the West Indies. They entered into a contract to serve and labour so long for so much money, and the children born to them in that condition were also held as bound to "service and labour." It also applies "indentured apprentices," and to persons taking upon themselves an obligation to "serve and labour." The constitution says that the party shall be delivered up to whom such service and labour may be due.

Why, sir, due!

In the first place this very clause of that provision makes it utterly impossible that it can apply to slaves. There is nothing due from the slave to his master in the way of service or labour. He is unable to show a contract.

The thing implies an arrangement, an understanding, by which, for an equivalent, I will do for you so much, if you will do for me, or have done for me, so much.

The constitution says he will be delivered up to whom any service or labour shall be due.

Due!

A slave owes nothing to any master; he can owe nothing to any master. In the eye of the law he is a chattel personal, to all intents, purposes, and constructions whatever.

Talk of a horse owing something to his master, or a sheep, or a wheel-barrow! Perfectly ridiculous!

The idea that a slave can owe anything!

I tell you what I would do if I were a judge; I could do it perfectly consistently with the character of the constitution. I have a proneness to liken myself to great people—to persons high in authority.

But if I were a judge, and a slave was brought before me under this provision of the constitution, and the master should insist upon my sending him back to slavery, I should inquire

I would point him to this same constitution, and tell him that I read in that constitution the great words of your own Magna Charta:—

"No person shall be deprived of life, liberty, or property without the process of law,"

and I ought to know by what contract, how this man contracted an obligation, or took upon himself to serve and labour for you.

And if he could not show that, I should dismiss the case and restore the man to his liberty. And I would do quite right, according to the constitution.

I admit nothing in favour of slavery when liberty is at stake; when I am called upon to argue on behalf of liberty I will range throughout the world, I am at perfect liberty by forms of law and by the roles of hermeneutics to range through the whole universe of God in proof of an innocent purpose, in proof of a good thing; but if you want to prove a bad thing, if you want to accomplish a bad and violent purpose, you must show it is so named in the bond. This is a sound legal rule.

Shakespeare noticed it as an existing rule of law in his "Merchant of Venice"; "a pound of flesh, but not one drop of blood."

The law was made for the protection of labour; not for the destruction of liberty; and it is to be presumed on the side of the oppressed.

The speaker at the City Hall laid down some rules of legal interpretation. These rules send us to the history of the law for its meaning.

I have no objection to this course in ordinary cases of doubt, but where human liberty and justice are at stake, the case falls under an entirely different class of rules. There must be something more than history, something more than tradition, to lead me to believe that law is intended to uphold and maintain wrong. The Supreme Court of the United States lays down this rule, and it meets the case exactly:

"Where rights are infringed; where the fundamental principles of the law are overthrown, where the general system of the law is departed from, the legislative intention must be expressed with irresistible clearness."

The same court says that the language of the law must be construed strictly in favour of justice and liberty; and another rule says, where the law is ambiguous and susceptible of two meanings, the one making it accomplish an innocent purpose, and the other making it accomplish a wicked purpose, we must in every case adopt that meaning which makes it accomplish an innocent purpose.

These are just the rules we like to have applied to us as individuals to begin with. We like to be assumed to be honest and upright in our purpose until we are proved to be otherwise, and the law is to be taken precisely in the same way. We are to assume it is fair, right, just, and true, till proved with irresistible power to be on the side of wrong.

Now, sir, a case like this occurred in Rhode Island some time ago. The people there made a law that no negro should be allowed to walk out after nine o'clock at night without a lantern. They were afraid the negro might be mistaken for somebody. The negroes got lanterns and walked after nine at night, but they forgot to put candles in them. They were arrested and brought before a court of law. They had been found after nine at night, it had been proved against them that they were out with lanterns to be sure, but without a candle.

"May it please your honour," it was argued for the prosecution, "of what value is a lantern without a candle? The plain intention of the law was that these people should not be out without a lantern and a candle."

But the judge said this was a law against the natural rights of man, against natural liberty, and that this law should be construed strictly. These men had complied with the plain reading of the law, and they must be dismissed

The judge in that case did perfectly right. The legislature had to pass another law, that no negro should be out after nine without a lantern and a candle in it. The negroes got candles, but forgot to light them. They were arrested again, again tried, and with a similar result.

There was then another law passed, that the negroes should not walk out after nine at night without lanterns, with candles in them, and the candles lighted. And if I had been a negro at that time in Rhode Island, I would have got a dark lantern and walked out.

Laws to sustain a wrong of any kind must be expressed with irresistible clearness; for law, be it remembered, is not an arbitrary rule of arbitrary mandate, and it has a purpose, a character in itself, a purpose of its own. Blackstone defines it as "a rule of the supreme power of the state;" but he does not stop there—he adds, "commanding that which is right, and forbidding that which is wrong"—that is law.

It would not be law if it commanded that which was wrong, and forbade that which was right in itself. It is necessary it should be on behalf of right.

There is another law of legal interpretation, which is, that the law is to be understood in the light of the objects sought for by the law, or sought in the law—that is, that the details of the law shall conform to the purpose declared to be sought to be attained by it. What are the objects sought for in the constitution of the American States?

"We, the people of these United States, in order to form a more perfect union, establish justice, ensure domestic tranquillity, provide for the common defence, promote the general welfare, and secure the blessings of liberty to ourselves and our posterity, do ordain and establish this constitution for the United States of America."

The objects here set forth are six in number. "Union" is one, not slavery; union is named as one of the objects for which the constitution was framed, and it is one that is very excellent; it is quite incompatible with slavery. "Defence" is another; "welfare" is another; "tranquillity" is another; "justice" and "liberty" are the others.

Slavery is not among them; the objects are union, defence, welfare, tranquillity, justice, and liberty.

Now, if the two last—to say nothing of the defence—if the two last purposes declared were reduced to practice, slavery would go reeling to its grave as if smitten with a bolt from heaven.

Let but the American people be true to their own constitution, true to the purposes set forth in that constitution, and we will have no need of a dissolution of the Union—we will have a dissolution of slavery all over that country.

But it has been said that negroes are not included in the benefits sought under this declaration of purposes.

Whatever slave-holders may say, I think it comes with ill grace from abolitionists to say the negroes in America are not included in this declaration of purposes.

The negroes are not included! Who says this?

The constitution does not say they are not included, and how dare any other person, speaking for the constitution, say so?

The constitution says "We the people;" the language is "we the people;" not we the white people, not we the citizens, not we the privileged class, not we the high, not we the low, not we of English extraction, not we of French or of Scotch extraction, but "we the people;" not we the horses, sheep, and swine, and wheelbarrows, but we the human inhabitants; and unless you deny that negroes are people, they are included within the purposes of this government.

They were there, and if we the people are included, negroes are included; they have a right, in the name of the constitution of the United States, to demand their liberty. This, I undertake to say, is the conclusion of the whole matter— that the constitutionality of slavery can be made out only by discrediting the plain, common sense reading of the constitution itself; by discrediting and casting away as worthless the most beneficent rules of legal interpretation; by ruling the negro outside of these beneficent rules; by claiming every thing for slavery; by denying every thing for freedom; by assuming that the constitution does not mean what it says; and that it says what it does not mean; by disregarding the written constitution; and interpreting it in the light of a secret understanding.

It is by this mean, contemptible, under-hand way of working out the pro-slavery character of the constitution, that the thing is accomplished, and in no other way. The first utterance of the instrument itself is gloriously on the side of liberty, and diametrically opposed to the thing called slavery in the United States.

The constitution declares that no person shall be deprived of life, liberty, or property without due process of law; it secures to every man the right of trial by jury; it also declares that the writ of habeas corpus shall never be suppressed—that great and noble writ—that writ by which England was made free soil—that writ which set Somerset free in 1772—that writ which made that land in which I stand tonight, and where you stand, the land of liberty and the home of the oppressed of all nations—the land of which Curran said when he spoke of it, that he spoke "in the spirit of the British law, which makes liberty commensurate with, and inseparable from, British soil; which proclaims even to the stranger and sojourner, the moment he sets his foot upon British earth, that the ground on which he treads is holy, and consecrated by the genius of universal emancipation."

It was in consequence of this writ—a writ which forms a part of the constitution of the United States—that England herself is free from man-hunters to-day; for in 1772 slaves were hunted here in England just as they are in America, and the British constitution was supposed to favour the arrest, the imprisonment, and re-capture of fugitive slaves. But Lord Mansfield, in the case of Somerset, decided that no slave could breathe in England.

We have the same writ, and let the people in Britain and the United States stand as true to liberty as the constitution is true to liberty, and we shall have no need of a dissolution of the Union.

But to all this it is said that the practice of the American people is against my view. I admit it. They have given the constitution a slaveholding interpretation. I admit it. And I go with him who goes furthest in denouncing these wrongs, these outrages on my people.

But to be consistent with this logic, where does it lead? Because the practice of the American people has been wrong, shall we therefore denounce the constitution?

The same logic would land the man of the City Hall precisely where the same logic has landed some of his friends in America—in the dark, benighted regions of infidelity itself.

The constitution is pro-slavery, because men have interpreted it to be pro-slavery, and practice upon it as if it were pro-slavery.

The very same thing, sir, might be said of the Bible itself; for in the United States men have interpreted the Bible against liberty. They have declared that Paul's epistle to Philemon is a full proof for the enactment of that hell-black Fugitive Slave Bill which has desolated my people for the last ten years in that country. They have declared that the Bible sanctions slavery.

What do we do in such a ease? What do you do when you are told by the slaveholders of America that the Bible sanctions slavery?

Do you go and throw your Bible into the fire? Do you sing out, "No Union with the Bible!"? Do you declare that a thing is bad because it has been misused, abused, and made a bad use of? Do you throw it away on that account?

No!

You press it to your bosom all the more closely; you read it all the more diligently; and prove from its pages that it is on the side of liberty—and not on the side of slavery.

So let us do so with the constitution of the United States. But this logic would carry the orator of the City Hall a step or two further; it would lead him to break down the British constitution. I believe he is not only a Protestant, but he is a Dissenter; and if he is opposed to the American constitution because certain evils exist therein, could he well oppose all the other constitutions?

But I must beg pardon for detaining you so long—I must bring my remarks speedily to a close.

Let me make a statement. It was said to you that the Southern States had increased from 5 up to 15. What is the fact with reference to this matter? Why, my friends, the slave States in America have increased just from 12 up to 15.

But the other statement was not told you. It is this: the Free States have increased from 1 up to 18. That fact was not told. No; I suppose it was expected I would come back and tell you all the truth. It takes two men to tell the truth any way.

The dissolution of the Union, remember, that was clamoured for that night, would not give the Northern states one single advantage over slavery that it does not now possess.

Within the Union we have a firm basis of opposition to slavery. It is opposed to all the great objects of the constitution. The dissolution of the Union is not only an unwise but a cowardly proposition. Dissolve the Union!

For what? Tear down the house in an instant because a few slates have been blown off the roof?

There are 350,000 slaveholders in America, and 26 millions of free white people. Must these 26 millions of people break up their government, dissolve their Union, burn up their constitution—for what? to get rid of the responsibility of holding slaves?

But can they get rid of responsibility by that? Alas no! The recreant husband may desert the family hearth, may leave his starving children, and you may place oceans, islands, and continents between him and his; but the responsibility, the gnawing of a guilty conscience must follow him wherever he goes.

If a man were on board of a pirate ship, and in company with others had robbed and plundered, his whole duty would not be performed simply by taking to the long boat and singing out, "No union with pirates!" His duty would be to restore the stolen property.

The American people in the Northern States have helped to enslave the black people.

Their duty will not have been done till they give them back their plundered rights. They cannot get rid of their responsibility by dissolving the Union; they must put down the evil, abolish the wrong. The abolition of slavery, not the dissolution of the Union, is the only way in which they can get rid of the responsibility.

"No union with slaveholding" is an excellent sentiment as showing hostility to slavery, but what is union with slavery? Is it living under the same sky, walking on the same earth, riding on the same railway, taking dinner on board of the same steamboat with the slaveholder?

No: I can be in all these relations to the slaveholder, but yet heaven-high above him, as wide from him as the poles of the moral universe.

"No union with slaveholding" is a much better phrase than that adopted by those who insist that they in America are the only friends of the slave who wish to destroy the Union.

Reference was made in the City Hall to my having held other views and different views from those I now entertain. An old speech of mine, delivered some fourteen years ago in London, was rendered with skill and effect.

I don't know what it was brought up for. Perhaps it was brought forward to show that I am not infallible, not like his reverence—of Rome.

If that was the object, I can relieve the friends of that gentleman entirely, by telling them that I never made any pretensions to infallibility.

Although I cannot accuse myself of being remarkably unstable, I cannot pretend that I have never altered my opinion both in respect to men and things.

Indeed I have been very much modified both in feeling and opinion within the last fourteen years, and he would be a queer man who could have lived fourteen years without having his opinions and feelings considerably modified by experience in that length of time.

When I escaped from slavery, twenty-two years ago, the world was all new to me, and if I had been in a hogshead with the bung in, I could not have been much more ignorant of many things then I was then.

I came out running. All I knew was that I had two elbows and a good appetite, and that I was a human being—a sort of nondescript creature, but still struggling for life.

The first I met were the Garrisonian abolitionists of Massachusetts. They had their views, opinions, platform, and eloquence, and were earnestly labouring for the abolition of slavery: They were my friends, the friends of my people, and nothing was more natural than that I should receive as gospel all they told me.

"When I was a child, I spake as a child, I understood as a child, I thought as a child; but when I became a man." —that is, after I went over to Great Britain and came back again—I undertook the herculean task, without a day's schooling, to edit and publish a paper—to unite myself to the literary profession.

I could hardly spell two words correctly; still I thought I could "join" as we say, and when I had to write three or four columns a week, it became necessary to re-examine some of the opinions I had formed in my baby days; and when I came to examine for myself my opinions were greatly modified, and I had the temerity to state to the parties from whom I received them my change of opinions; and from that day to this—whether in the east or the west, in or out of America, in Ireland, Scotland, or England—I have been pursued and persecuted by that class of persons on account of my change of opinions.

But I am quite well satisfied, very well satisfied with my position.

Now, what do I propose? what do you propose? what do we sensible folks propose?—for we are sensible. The slaveholders have ruled the American government for the last fifty years; let the anti-slavery party rule the nation for the next fifty years.

And, by the way, that thing is on the verge of being accomplished .

The slave-holders, above all things else, dread the rule of the anti-slavery party that are now coming into power. To dissolve the Union would be to do just what the slaveholders would like to have done.

Slavery is essentially a dark system; all it wants is to be excluded and shut out from the light.

If it can only be boxed in where there is not a single breath to fall upon it, nor a single word to assail it, then it can grope in its own congenial darkness, oppressing human hearts and crushing human happiness.

But it dreads the influence of truth; it dreads the influence of Congress. It knows full well that when the moral sentiment of the nation shall demand the abolition of slavery, there is nothing in the constitution of the United States to prevent that abolition.

Well, now, what do we want? We want this:—whereas slavery has ruled the land, now must liberty; whereas pro-slavery men have sat in the Supreme Court of the United States, and given the constitution a pro-slavery interpretation against its plain reading, let us by our votes put men into that Supreme Court who will decide, and who will concede, that that constitution is not slavery.

What do you do when you want reform or change? Do you break up your government?

By no means. You say:—"Reform the government;" and that is just what the abolitionists who wish for liberty in the United States propose.

They propose that the intelligence, the humanity, the Christian principle, the true manliness which they feel in their hearts, shall flow out from their hearts through their fingers into the ballot-box, and that into that ballot-box it shall go for such men as shall represent the Christian principle and Christian intelligence in the United States, and that congress shall crystallise those sentiments into law, and that law shall be in favour of freedom.

And that is the way we hope to accomplish the abolition of slavery.

Since these questions are put here, it is a bounden duty to listen to arguments of this sort; and I know that the intelligent men and women here will be glad to have this full exposé of the whole question.

I thank you very sincerely for the patient attention you have given me.

CPSIA information can be obtained
at www.ICGtesting.com
Printed in the USA
BVOW06s2249120217
475956BV00006B/92/P